A book that can change your attitude towards life.

WIN THE BATTLE OF CONFLICTS WITHIN

Ways of Surviving the Tsunami of Mind

RAM SHANKER TIWARI

Published by:

F-2/16, Ansari road, Daryaganj, New Delhi-110002
☎ 23240026, 23240027 • *Fax:* 011-23240028
info@vspublishers.com • www.vspublishers.com

Online Brandstore: amazon.in/vspublishers

Regional Office : Hyderabad
5-1-707/1, Brij Bhawan (Beside Central Bank of India Lane)
Bank Street, Koti, Hyderabad - 500 095
☎ 040-24737290
vspublishershyd@gmail.com

Follow us on:   

BUY OUR BOOKS FROM: AMAZON FLIPKART

ISBN 978-93-813847-8-7

New Edition

Printed at : Param Offsetters, Okhla, New Delhi–110020

Dedication

Dedicated to the Lotus feet of my Guruji
Reverend Shri Shāntānand ji Puri
of Vashishtha Guhā, Himālaya.

Why This Book?

Night of 26 December, 2004. I was travelling by Tamil Nadu express, with my family. We nine members of the party were heading towards Chennai; from there we had a plan to go to Tirupati by bus. It was 3'O clock in the morning; all were fast asleep; the train was running with high speed towards south. Suddenly, the mobile phone of my son, Rajesh, rang. Dinesh, my son-in-law, was speaking from Bhopal: "Wherever you people are, get off the train at the next stoppage, don't go to Chennai; a raging hurricane is lashing that region. Thousands of people have been killed".

Outer Upheavals

Chennai was still about four hours away. We hurriedly packed and got down at the next station: Gudur. After sometime, we talked to the local people, saw the morning newspaper, then we came to know that an oceanic typhoon –named Tsunami, is raging at the southern sea coast. It had engulfed a wide area, from northern region of Australia up to the Indian coasts of the southern peninsula.

We proceeded to Tirupati by road from Gudur. While worshipping Lord Venkatesh, a thought flashed in my mind – "O God! Why such thunderbolt of trauma on the simple, innocent, poor people: children, women, elderly persons, and innumerable helpless beings? Why has this fierce dance of death and destruction descended?"

After four days of this havoc, we visited Marina Beach of Chennai where we could see the muddy and bloody paws of tsunami!

Inner Upheavals

In life also, the upheaval of tornado occurs, at some stage or the other, when our emotions, sentiments, instincts, and conflicts get compactly deposited in the unconscious layer of mind, and when extreme pressure, tensions and turmoil are activated, then the strata of mental structure start cracking, tearing apart and rupturing. Then, opens the floodgate of emotions, high-rise waves of anger and hatred and attack of fear devastatingly destroy the mental peace and happiness. We get lost in melancholy, clutched in depression and drowned in sludge of hopelessness. We throw away our *Gāndeev*. Our life appears to be worthless, and existence purposeless. The death seems to be dearer than life – even if enormous prosperity is wedded to us!

I have also faced the trauma of tsunamis in my life – from childhood: once or twice faced a situation of loss in totality, hand-shake with the god of death, insult, infamy, betrayal and pain of immense dejection. But fortunately my philosophy and spirituality supported me and I survived.

Treatises of Wisdom

Cultural background of the childhood, contacts with the wise, faith in God, scientific approach and structure of positive *karma* – all these forces of positivity have always helped me to liberate myself from the mire of bad times. After retirement from service, I started reading and contemplating upon various wisdom treatises of the world. I could dive into philosophy, psychology, religion and spirituality as treasured by the glorious sages and the wise of the east as well as the western analysts of Upanishads, lights of Buddha, Christ, Descartes, Patanjali, Formulators of Tao and Zen – the golden essence of ken and enlightenment of all. I could avail my freedom to analyze and synthesize the fundamental organizations of atheism and theism, science and religion and the complexity of human mind and thoughts.

Thereafter, I dived into the celestial waters of *Gitā-Gnyān,* the wisdom of the Gitā. The Gitā is the axis of my existence. I could deeply dissect and analyze every religious and spiritual phenomenon with the sharp knife of cause and effect, which was possible because of my training in science. Then my first book – *The Yoga of Gitā*, originated. By now, I was totally out of my life-long sphere of research in plant-and-earth sciences; expanding the newer circle of my being, I continued to swim in the bliss of the real knowledge.

In continuum, two more books- *The Four Stroke Success* and *The Reality of Personal God* saw the light of the day.

Our Treatises of Wisdom, belonging to some religious philosophy are studded with gems of human welfare and blessings, but their language generally weaves simile, metaphors, allegory, comparisons and indicative symbols. At times, their literary meanings may produce droughts and confusion; the word-for-word sense does not usher into any clear pathway. But if they could be perceived or redesigned, and symbolic formations on their subtle intimation could be elucidated or construed, then these fountains of divine wisdom could flow as pristine stream of ecstasy and bliss; such as the secret of the Gitā.

Wish to Share

I want to share the views which have been expressed in the book with the young generation of the time, and also with those who negate our ancient treasure of knowledge or who want to see god on the basis of cause and effect only. Even to them, I wish to convey my ideas who are hard-core fatalistic, or those who disintegrate at the time of distress.

The ups-and-downs in life will come in continuum. Do not be terrorized by them. Try to decipher their frame-work. Even before the high waves rise, understand the signals and signs and then intently subdue the upheavals of thoughts. Had we shared the wisdom with animals the loss of life in the tsunami would have been the minimum.

Identify and destroy each point of tension in day-to-day living. Intensive observation, tranquil awareness, and discriminative intellect are the tools for such achievements of stress-free life. Don't allow to build up the load of clutter and accumulate it. Diffuse the stress as well as strain! Disperse them and make them ineffective! Subdue the troubles of mind! We go on agitating because everything goes on changing, always changing; try to understand the ever-changing phenomena in the world and also the jumping nature of mind. However, even then the tsunami may strike hard but it can't destroy the serenity, stability and calmness of life. Such a balanced state could be achieved only through knowledge: complete ken!

Acknowledgements

I am grateful to Dinesh, Anita, Sanjay, Swati, Rajesh, Seema and Vishnukanta for lovingly enquiring, off-and-on, about the progress of my only job – the scribbling, which got entangled in the 'writer's block' for about two years. This was mainly due to the publisher-writer syndrome, so often experienced by most of the writers. Desperately, I withdrew with a sense of de-motivation. But, it was an experience in itself for which I am thankful to the concerned firm for keeping my manuscript for 15 months and then returning with regret. This incident, though a peril, showed me the path anew to walk on and on!

In December, 2007, I happened to sit at the holy feet of my Gurudev. Earlier, I had understood him saying that at certain stage in life, one should lay all his activities except *Sādhnā*. This in my mind, I requested Guruji if I were to continue writing on my favourite subject: spirituality, science, psychology; with a view to cater younger generation. Venerable Gurudev very lovingly explained: "What you are doing is a righteous *karma* not desiring money, fame, name or reward; it is helpful particularly to the youth who urgently need some spiritual guidance, founded on scientific reasoning."

“Go ahead”, he sanctified, “and my best blessings are with you!”

So it all re-started.

How do I express my indebtedness to the mentor of my life in all directions of my existence? My loving surrender to his holy feet!

The present book is the English transcription of the author’s latest book: “Sukh Avam Shānti: Kab, Kahān aur Kaise?”

Contents

Preface 13

Introduction 23

1. Tsunami of Mind 29
   - (a) Symphony – 1 42
   - (b) Resonance – 1 55
   - (c) Take in a Stride – 1 57
2. Dimensions of Unhappiness 58
   - (a) Symphony - 2 75
   - (b) Resonance – 2 87
   - (c) Take in a Stride – 2 88
3. Structure of Karma 90
   - (a) Symphony – 3 105
   - (b) Resonance – 3 117
   - (c) Take in a Stride – 3 119

4. Meditation: The Gateway to Freedom ________ 120
   (a) Symphony – 4 ________ 140
   (b) Resonance – 4 ________ 153
   (c) Take in a Stride – 4 ________ 154
5. Pathways to Enlightenment ________ 156
   (a) Symphony – 5 ________ 170
   (b) Resonance – 5 ________ 182
   (c) Take in a Stride – 5 ________ 183
6. Infinite Energy of the Cosmos ________ 185
   (a) Symphony – 6 ________ 200
   (b) Resonance – 6 ________ 210
   (c) Take in a Stride – 6 ________ 211
7. Ascent of Spiritual Evolution ________ 212
   (a) Symphony – 7 ________ 225
   (b) Resonance – 7 ________ 234
   (c) Take in a Stride – 7 ________ 235
8. Towards Nirvāna: Freedom....! ________ 236
   (a) Symphony – 8 ________ 250
   (b) Resonance – 8 ________ 258
   (c) Take in a Stride – 8 ________ 260

Preface

Violent Cyclone of Sufferings

Human mind can be ideally happy, in continuum, when all its desires are fulfilled and when one's life attains a zero-agitation state. Desires, longings or thirsty tendencies multiply according to geometrical ratio: two to four, four to sixteen, sixteen to two hundred fifty six (16 x 16), and then infinitude! Such is the arithmetic of our sensuous hunger. But, alas! The desires can never be satiated totally, and this perpetual incompleteness makes us miserable, injecting the pain of void in our veins. Even in dreams! We may have fabulous wealth and ineffable power, yet depression, turmoil, worry, angst and unclassified emptiness do not leave chasing us frantically. Therefore, it is essential to discriminately understand the infrastructure of melancholy, grief, unhappiness and frustration (cumulatively known as *Klesha*). The equation of happiness and unhappiness is pivoted upon the ratio of non-attachment and intense desires!

Every elemental existence in the world is changing every split second. The only unchangeable phenomenon is the process of ever-and-ever change! Leaving other aspects apart, our mind, ego and the so-called intelligence are also undergoing rapid alteration.

We are unable to stop quivering of an electron, what to talk of the worldly systems or nature's wheel of whirlpool! The platform on which the life exists is revolving whereupon we creatures are dancing. Both are mobile – the stage as well as the actors. Non-stationary! Upon that, the future and purpose of all this melodrama is ambiguous, unknowable. Now, it is pitch darkness. Now, it is brilliant light! In a moment – a soothing melody; the other moment it is ear-piercing screeching agony and clutter of irritating drumming! And, dance! We have to, because this is the *modus operandi* of passion and attachment; tantrum of 'sensuous excitement and pleasure'. So is the magnetic force of desires and mélange of ignorance: the cosmic illusion. Confused, confounded, bewildered, stunned we go on living like vegetable or, at the most, like a dog: hounding, searching for something rotten to eat, wrapped in sensuality, fighting, snarling, barking, and howling! And in the end, when death knocks at our door, we turn to be empty, trembling, unfulfilled and absolute broke. We had all the luxury but no cognizance of the Self, no dispassion, no discriminative power to sort out the real from the unreal; resultantly, we convolute in the sludge of our private, personal hell, sinking in the mire of agony, fear and a total loss.

What a life!

Then, what shall we do?

Is there a way to fulfillment?

How to dance in symphony?

The key to such and similar questions lies in our own "personality", in our attitude towards life; nowhere else! Distinctive characteristic – the wholeness of being – is a dynamic system which acts through mind, intellect and ego as well as the physical form. The personality, thus structured as a complex mechanism, synchronizes with the environment: the social, emotional, natural and intellectual set up in which a person exists. In other words, every person possesses a unique personality – being the only one of its kind, driven by the totality of thought-complex and bodily system; every person has different methodology to deal with his or her own world; some psychologists opine that this uniqueness represents an expression of *unconscious* mind through the *conscious* mind. It is the striking quality of each person. The ego plays a vital role in such an expression which awakens the sleeping desires.

Structure of the Ego

The ego develops in the field of unconscious mind but remains activated in the region of conscious mind. It is helping as well as, at times, antagonist, too. It creates instinct within for our survival to motivate us for defensive mode and worthy activities, but if the ego goes berserk and surges in rage, it may create hellish hot situation for us.

The ego and unconscious level of thoughts construct our personality. The ego is an alert and awakened factor of our mind-thought-complex. We become happy or unhappy because of our ego. All our activities, actions and fruitions thereof can be understood with respect to ego.

If we are able to develop an emotionally stable, tranquil, calm and middle-path-walker ego, our road of progress towards happiness and peace gets facilitated. It becomes a thoroughfare.

Almost all religions, faiths and philosophies had been preaching, since millennia, to get rid of worldly illusion and to weed out rampant desires so that happiness and bliss could dawn at the dark horizons of human life; that is, to walk on the illumined path of self-knowledge. But the more we walk in this realm, the more we are hindered in evolving our being. Wars, conflicts, human agony, terrorism, selfishness, corruption, deterioration of environment and *karma* of negativity seem to be incessantly increasing. The nature has very kindly bestowed us unrestricted freedom to think, to express and to act: liberty of thought, speech and action! No other animate being enjoys such a boon of boundless faculties. But, we the humans forget that with this freedom come immense responsibilities also. Regretfully, we utilize our right of freedom – in positive or negative manner to fulfill our desires – but generally we do not abide by moral accountability of our actions. We have to be immensely responsible towards the society, Nature and the Self-being. Consequently, not doing so, we mostly remain in a state of turmoil and void, insufficiency, unsatisfied, unstableness, alarmed, frightened and unfulfilled.

Who is responsible for such a misfortune?

How to get out of this slime and slush?

Where is immutable bliss?

Self-Attainment

Man has created such a misery for himself. Humans have themselves become the pallbearer of their own peace and happiness. Yet by way of self-attainment we can escape this bog of sludge. Self-attainment or self-realization (*Āatma bodh*) has a vast connotation. Here we are not adopting its metaphysical, religious or supra-mental meaning because such concepts could be the cause of division, isolation or contradiction. The religion with a meaning of blinkered view divides the humanity; it can never unite. Unity of love and apathy requires an innocent thinking and stainless actions; narrow definition of our faiths does not have that.

In the present context, thus, the self-attainment circumscribes self-evolution, enrichment of our inbeing and achievement of discriminative power to sort out the truth from the non-truth.

Satisfaction in material accumulation,
Stabilization of mind and intellect,
Creative thought-flow,
Searching meaning of life,
Sync in attitude,
Softness in manners,
Unblemished heart, like that of a child,
Sense of personal responsibility,
Enthusiasm in duty,
Absence of craving for extravagant needs,
Connectedness with the Creator.

Such a plan for self-ascent may bring an experience of bliss. The mind calms down in the transcendental state. The dreaded load of the past is taken off from head and the fear of uncertainty vanishes. A soft flow of experiences makes the mind serene: to face challenges in life, to earn life-supporting prosperity, to walk in the realm of delight, happiness, satisfaction and bliss, to get rid of clutter and prejudices, and to be liberated from fear of death: for such attainment we have to consciously make vigorous efforts!

Then, afterwards where remains a need of searching the ultimate, immutable happiness? It is in the karma, in the attitude towards happenings around us and in the vital force to do meritorious action: rightfully earn prosperity, live naturally, enjoy judiciously and withdraw from attachment intelligently!

Outside the periphery of ritualistic religious system, the Gitā is an eternal spring of knowledge which makes the personality shine, guides to succeed in self-actualization and connects one to the Absolute. The aforesaid eleven points of self-attainment are the boons of Gitā which in modern times are narrated variedly in new wrappers!

In the current era, the teachings of Gitā are urgently required for applying brakes on rampant deterioration of character, increasing crimes, violence, deceit, dishonesty glittering allurements, greed for sensuousness, crisis of faithfulness, depreciation of original love, and decadence in human relationships. Gitā can salvage the humanity and rescue intelligent species of *Homo sapiens* because it is a time-tested universal science of human thought, speech and action. Even after the lapse of thousands of years, the freshness of this knowledge and force of its conviction remain in the ascendant because this enlightenment is structured upon human psychology which analyses the basic organization of universal traits common to all races, countries, regions, creeds or colours. Hence these gems of wisdom are trans-global. The timeless teachings of Gitā are the essence of *Vedas* and *Upanishads*. Sri Krishna, the Narrator, is the Royal Yogi, (*Yogishwar*), ever established in the Yoga, hence his pronouncement is taken as the expression of the Cosmic Energy: the Truth, Immortal, Awareness, and Absolute Bliss: the *Brahman*; the Voice of the Creator!

This is the attainment of the Absolute through the path of self- actualization!

The Rainbow of Fulfillment

"Things" around us in the world do not have any quality; they do not create any characteristic by themselves, rather it is our mind (a product of our brain) which incessantly fabricates qualities of things; the brain through stimuli, relayed by our sense organs, does this magic. Therefore, we must continuously organize our experiences which flow non-stop out of the non-stable world. We must also winnow and assort input data in accordance with their utility for attaining the goal of our life. Our mind creates our world continuously, day and night, till we breathe last. At the same time our determination generates our *karma.* It is a tragedy that against the backdrop of our desires as well as innate tendencies, we go on searching a meaning of our coming on this planet, called earth, and in self-illusion we feel a sense of false fulfillment, in painful labour, futile attempts to engorge our wild desires; we take it for granted, though erroneously, that the aim of life is to satisfy our longings and it is the only purpose of our existence. But we forget that when we search happiness in the limited territory of selfishness, it always eludes us. A perpetual feeling of well-being and contentment can only be achieved through disciplined, balanced mind but not by an intoxicated, jumping and erratic one, always manipulating for its own agenda.

1. The Gitā declares

युञ्जन्नेवं सदात्मानं योगी नियतमानसः।
शान्तिं निर्वाणपरमां मत्संस्थामधिगच्छति।।

(6:15)

In this way, always keeping the mind in balance, the yogi practicing the control of thoughts enters the eternal peace which has its abode in My nature, and such a yogi attaining the ultimate bliss is liberated totally.

The final target of complacency is the freedom, the *Moksha,* the *Nirvāna*, release from bondages, dispassion and eternal tranquility. The Gitā meticulously takes out the embedded thorns from the human mind. This knowledge cuts the complex knots of our subconscious existence. Such tumors are painful albeit we might have taken them as benedictory. The light of Gitā ushers into such a path by walking on which we can survive the tornado generated by the Tsunami of our mind. In spite of this, it is your decision as to which policy you do adopt: benevolent or non-moral. Yet what hinders you to stride along some distance on the pathway of the Gitā?

This is a pristine experience, not a ritualistic practice! This is an absolute awareness, not merely dry informative data. By the Realization of the Self we may ultimately be granted Freedom.

2. The Gitā Opines Assertively on the Issue of Awareness

श्रेयान्द्रव्यमयाद्यज्ञाज्ज्ञानयज्ञः परंतप।
सर्वं कर्माखिलं पार्थ ज्ञाने परिसमाप्यते।।

(4:33)

Superior is "Knowledge-sacrifice" to "Sacrifice-with-object", O Parantapa! All actions in their entirety, O Pārtha! Culminate in Knowledge.

Knowledge is more spiritual and *Sāttvik* than all the rituals. To burn ignorance in the fire of knowledge is known as *Gyān Yagya*. We destroy the knots of our unconscious by the awareness of the truth; then only we may enter the Kingdom of Eternal Peace. Such awareness trickles down from the spring of Gitā.

In the present book, along with *Gitā Gyān*, the principles of psychology and general science have also been assimilated. Where does lie the root of our unhappiness, although we are well-off materially? How to come out of this ditch? As spiritual as well as practical answers the chapters to follow have been structured upon *Meditation*, *Energy of the Cosmos*, *Pathway to Enlightenment, Ultimate Freedom, Dimensions of Unhappiness,* and other peripheral regimen. It is hoped, fresh perspective will make some newer ideas to sprout in the mind of the reader. It is a well-established fact that a tiniest change in life begets a commendable success in due course. Try to make a subtle change today. It may rise to be a colossal Himalaya of ascent after a few years!

We have learnt in this lesson:

Desires as well as scenario of the world go on changing every moment; obviously, to satiate the desires is an impossible equation.

The secret of our contentment and complete gratification lies embedded in our personality as well as our view point.

Peace and happiness can be attained only by training our ego to be worthy of our existence.

By self-attainment or by real gain of advantage, we may search for a satisfied state, tranquil happiness, stability, fulfillment, un-spoilt mind and the meaning of our life.

We may survive unscratched from the onslaught attacks of modern absurdities, by practising the wisdom of Gitā.

To keep a critical balance of mind in all ups-and-downs in life is possible only by the unadulterated wisdom.

You can live a superior life than what you are living now! Think!

Listen to and follow what Sri Krishna said:

For a self-disciplined yogi, there exists an absolute freedom prevailing in his life; such yogis can never be in bondage by anger and unsatisfied longings; they control their thoughts from going haywire, and ultimately realize the Brahman.

The Gitā (5:26)

Introduction

The Divine Song of Action

गीता सुगीता कर्तव्या किमन्यैः शास्त्रविस्तरैः।
या स्वयं पद्मनाभस्यः मुखपद्माद्विनिःसृता।।

One must contemplate and thoroughly reflect upon the teachings of Gitā; then other treatises of knowledge are not required because the Gitā has been directly narrated by Lord Krishna Himself.

Mahabharat, Bhisma Parva 43 (1)

The Srimadbhagwad Gitā is a divine poetry in which love, devotion, action, grace and philosophy of life as well as creation have been harmoniously synthesized. This is an art of living and a science of fulfillment. It has been accepted and lauded by all: both from east and west:

Comparatively, our modern world and its literature appear to be insignificant and of little worth. **Henery Thory**

It is an experience as if a Kingdom is addressing to us; nothing is small or superfluous, rather all is grand, serene and immutable ...! **Emerson**

The Gitā is a bouquet composed of the beautiful flowers of spiritual truths collected from the Upanishads.

Swami Vivekananda

The Gitā is one of the clearest and most comprehensive summaries of the perennial philosophy ever to have been done. Hence it's enduring value, not only for Indians, but for all mankind... The Bhāgavadgitā is perhaps the most systematic spiritual statement of the perennial philosophy. **Aldous Huxley**

The Gitā is the *Vedānta*: the essence of *Vedas* and *Upanishads*; the elixir extracted from the pristine knowledge of *Vedas*. In Hindu religion, it is the nuclear scripture. Through the flow of millennia, all the faiths of the world, which were subsequently founded, have imbibed several aspects of the Gitā in varied forms; the golden brilliance of the Gitā thus spread all-over the world, not remaining restricted to one religion or one geographic region. This knowledge has become an integral part of the philosophy of humanity and the human clan in totality.

In the unique dialogue of Gitā, all fundamental systems of faiths and their basic structures have been reflected; it is a synthesis of universal wisdom by adapting to which a balanced way of living could be achieved. Hence, the Gitā can never be delimited within the framework of time-space. With regard to its universality, the Gitā must be understood as 'spiritual psychology', because innate tendency of human beings exhibits inborn leaning towards achieving divine characters. The Gitā puts forth such a device which instigates our mind to search the Reality of Existence, to comprehend the Primordial Power, and to enter the unknown dimensions of the human mind. By walking on the path enlightened by the Gitā, we become capable of strengthening our convictions and evolving our values of life; this enriches our experiences. Our turmoil and upheavals are pacified, and there comes a serene synchronization between our life-style and the existence.

Gitā's greatness does not require any favourable judgment from us; it means, the wisdom is pre-eminently celestial and radiantly brilliant; whether we sing a song in its appreciation or not, the Gitā remains eternally graceful and elegant. Yet, in spite of this, we try to imbibe its blissful, splendid beauty in our being.

Lord Krishna Himself narrates in admiration of the Gitā:

वेदेषु यज्ञेषु तपःसु चैव दानेषु यत्पुण्यफलं प्रदिष्टम्।
अत्येति तत्सर्वमिदं विदित्वा योगी परं स्थानमुपैति चाद्यम्।।

(8:28)

Yogi, knowing this secret, transcends beyond the fruits which one is bestowed by the study of Vedas and from performance of sacrifices, austerity, devotion, or charity, etc. Such a yogi gets absolved from the cycle of life and death and establishes in the highest abode of the Lord, attaining the Supreme.

In other words, the Gitā recognizes Yoga as the best path for achieving knowledge. Study of religious treatises, austerity and liberal donations are also established means to gain spiritual experience, no doubt, but the one who follows the path of meditation surpasses all others; his mind achieves permanent tranquility, serenity, and equanimity. By way of meditation one gets all supernatural capabilities in unobstructed manner – without troublesome efforts, unlike other paths. The truth remains that by adopting the technique of yoga, the personality of the devotee blossoms forth and ultimately all his desires, tendencies and conceptual prejudices are melted and infused into the realm of peace.

The power of discriminative intellect expands the consciousness of a yogi. And, in the end, such an adept achieves self-awareness which is the abode of the Absolute. On the way, such a practitioner does not get entangled into agitation created by desires for fruition of his efforts.

Evidently, the Gitā is the original fountain of Yoga. It is a dynamic supporter to achieve the goal of happiness in life.

In the last chapter of the Gitā, while summing up, Sri Krishna takes Arjuna to the subtlest level of this wisdom; He says that without a thorough cleansing of one's mind, it would be an attempt in futility to comprehend or to practise this path; it may not yield benediction to a fifthly, cluttered mind.

इदं ते नातपस्काय नाभक्ताय कदाचन।
न चाशुश्रूषवे वाच्यं न च मां योऽभ्यसूयति।।

(18:67)

This is never to be spoken by you to one who is devoid of austerities or devotion, not to one who does not render service, not to one who desires not to listen, not to one who cavils at Me.

This statement points out that an intensive faith and unshakable belief is mandatory for imbibing this wisdom. In addition, there must not be any conflict or doubt in the mind of the seeker. One must be benevolent, wishing to do good, actively friendly and helpful and charitable; one must be inquisitive for seeking knowledge and a rock-believer in the supremacy of the Almighty. Only such aspirant may be totally blessed with the approbation from Above.

श्रद्धावाननसूयश्च शृणुयादपि यो नरः।
सोऽपि मुक्तः शुभाँल्लोकान्प्राप्नुयात्पुण्यकर्मणाम्।।

गीता (18:71)

That man also, who hears this, full of faith and without malice, he too, liberated, shall attain to the happy worlds of those righteous deeds.

Faith is that faculty of human intellect by which subtle meanings of spiritual sagacity and *Viveka* could be understood. There remains no place for doubt, uncertainty or emptiness when our heart is filled with unquestioned trust and belief. The faith comes to flowering when there is a total intellectual surrender at the altar of the Almighty.

Another necessary factor includes non-resistance, lack of disgust or disliking. No hindrance should be created by our mind in the continuous flow of the knowledge; no blockade in the stream of wisdom: as it trickles down naturally, let it play freely. Then only we will be able to quench our thirst for knowledge.

In the modern context, we are subjected to slavery of absurdities around us. We feel rejected and dejected amid the explosion of our unfulfilled desires. Consequently, we are caught up in the violent cycle of depression. Although affluence weds us, in the end we experience a total defeat.

Yet, the Gitā promises:

यत्र योगेश्वरः कृष्णो यत्र पार्थो धनुर्धरः।
तत्र श्रीर्विजयो भूतिर्ध्रुवा नीतिर्मतिर्मम।।

(18:78)

Wherever is Krishna, the Yogiraj, wherever is Partha, the archer, there are prosperity, victory, happiness, and steady policy; this is my conviction.

This fact was expressed by Sanjay who was narrating details of Mahabharata war to the blind king Dhritarāshtra. Sri Krishna was established in Yoga, completely unified with the dynamic Awareness, righteously a sharp analyst, and prudent performer of action *(Karmayogi)*; Arjuna was an invincible warrior, courageous fighter, calm and intelligent prince. Thus, according to Sanjay, the victory had to be on the side of Sri Krishna and Arjuna.

If you wish to earn prosperity, virtuous bases of action, contentment, and ultimate freedom *(moksha)* encompassed by the melody of happiness and peace, you must cultivate characteristics of Sri Krishna and Arjuna, Yogishwar and Yogi – maybe in minuscule degrees, to start with, because: *Yogi is always happy and contended; he neither grieves for someone, nor expects something for himself.*

Summary:

Almost similar mentality pervades through the minds of humans, all-over the world. This is a natural trait.

Toiling to 'have' abundance in excessive materialism, we usually become empty.

We don't 'be' abundant.

We search for support of mutable, not that of the immutable.

Ancient wisdom extends powerful support to us to solve the problems of our life.

The Gitā is the in-affable edition of wisdom.

Knowledge can never be imbibed without faith.

Tranquility can never be achieved without knowledge.

Where does fulfillment lie without inner peace?

Hate germinates conflict.

There is confusion in rituals and fanaticism.

Where there are dynamic awareness and action, there are prosperity and moral rectitude.

Patience, kindness and incessant judicious actions lead to well-being and autonomy.

Yet we have many pertinent questions:

How can we survive the agony and worries in this world, and how can we escape the turmoil of mental tsunami cyclones in life? How can the psychological approach of the Gitā help us in this battle with emotional typhoons?

We shall see satisfactory answers in the following pages.

Tsunami of Mind

Tsunami is a Japanese word which is used for the horrid death-dance of oceanic waves created by violent tornado and torrent of wind, and downpour of rain. It is a vault and salutation of annihilation: sea waves appear to engulf the sky; tidal force breaks the barrier of sea-shore and invades the dwelling, encroaching miles of land; cataclysm occurs in a wide-spread region; high velocity wind rages and unimaginable destruction giggles. Several ships, boats, plants and vegetation, houses and hutments, and inhabitants of countryside, animals, creatures and birds – all come in the clutches of body-thirsty Tsunami. Life structure at sea as well as nearby land is shattered and strewn far-and-wide, like a palace of straw. Loss of life, property and ecology happens to be incalculable. Holocaust, trauma, the great doom!

In the month of December, 2004, a furious tsunami had struck the south-eastern region of Asia – it is known to all. Also, in the current year tsunami has struck again at many areas of Pacific shore. The geo-scientists say that such havoc occurs because of subsurface movements of rocks under the oceanic bed. Extensive 'cracks' are developed below in the crust under the water-body – the mega-cracks which can swallow huge mountains! Subsequently, earthquakes are triggered off and the crust of the earth expands a little, disturbing the critical balance of the geo-dynamics in that region. As a result, the ocean 'boils' up. Lofty waves try to engulf the sky.

Tsunami does not occur at defined interval of time, hence it's unpredictable: Erratic! Whenever and wherever a tension develops in the layers of sediments, it results into pull, push and thrust therein, and, at times, the flow of lava, deep down in the earth, increases; then the blanket of the earth below the sea-bed becomes uneasy, agitated and full of turmoil, causing tsunami, disturbing even the atmosphere.

In the minds of human beings also, such bustles, violent disruptions, agitations, churning and confusion occur from time to time, but at some point of crisis, devastating uncertainty prevails in life. These are the *'Tsunamis of mind'*: created by tension, anxiety, discontent, anger, passion, hate, attachment, and so on; an uncontrolled, excited state of mind is created, thus. Obviously, at such point, an analysis of mind as well as that of the causal factors of uneasiness is urgently required. Then only our query about "Happiness and peace: when, where and how?" could be answered; and we may win the battle of conflicts within.

Multi-Dimensional Mind

Our own mind creates our own world: the one we comprehend. Our societal and cultural background also shapes our experiences – generally similar, but in different ways. Either we take the 'things' for granted as real, or we define them on the basis of shared experiences, our education, civilization, etc., but still they are only some sketch diagrams drawn by our own mind. Our mind always remains over-busy in the expanse of 'reasons', emotions and sensuality. These realms are unlimited in their extent of spreading and, like a chameleon, change their colours every moment. Our mind also dances on the rhythm of our ego – now happy, now unhappy, satisfied … unsatisfied…! But the happiness is momentary because the ego goes on searching for ever anew circles of indulgence. Despite the material luxury, dark clouds of agony (desire) bedeck our mind again and again. In such a situation, where can we find the eternal peace and immutable, absolute bliss?

If a person identifies his own deficiency and lack of moral excellence, the royal road to divine experience gets opened for higher achievement.

Our convictions and values of life indicate the horizon of our thoughts.

We must not become intimate with the thirst and hunger for sensuous gratification. This relationship should remain at the level of indifference so that self-discipline could germinate in our being.

Self-control gives rise to practical intellect by which we become capable of taking undistorted decision, and work for evolving cardinal virtues without hindrances.

Diversity of Mind

A continuous inflow of absurdities through media corrupts our thoughts and values; it stimulates feeling of crime, violence and sensuality. Ugly aspect of alien culture has entered our sitting room which instigates our unfulfilled desires. One can very well see the result of such an onslaught attack of filth on our societal structure: crime, killing, rape, consumerism, emptiness and out of proportion increase in negativity! Then, in addition, our mind has a characteristic, or it is its weakness, that once it tastes 'blood' it doesn't leave the habit. The mind has enormous power; once it is caught up in vicious circle, our intellect also becomes a helpless onlooker – unable to control it. Unwarranted habit makes the mind a bonded slave.

Our mind always seeks some sort of pleasure, the desire of which makes it miserable. A longing for experiencing enjoyment, excitement becomes violent, at times, but the pleasure-related happiness cannot be defined easily. It has multiple meanings. What are the basic elements of a happy life? If things which we craze for, and which conform to our wild desires happen in continuity – without a break – we are happy. Otherwise we are not. We remain miserable. Wealth, pleasant friendship, harmonious family life, satisfaction in sensuality, health, job of liking with a fat salary, prestige in society… and so on! But even then, the real happiness cannot be given an exact meaning. The more we eat, the more we crave. Then we abhor; the greater the indulgence, the higher the detestation. If we fill our belly up to our throat, no delicacy or highly pleasing food can serve happiness on our platter. And, above all, every moment the systems and arrangements of desires as well as 'things' go on changing in the world outside; and inside our thought-chamber as well!

They say, we can't enter the same river again, i.e., when you enter for the second time, by that moment the river will be changed, and you, too. The alteration in every aspect of life goes on with great speed; we may or may not feel it. In such a revolution of systems, where lies the real happiness, where is permanent peace?

We have to be alert and aware about this confused horse-race in our mind. Aware, in continuum in the present moment! To live for 'today', for this hour, the past is over; one can learn from experience. The future is an uncertainty; one may plan in a casual way about the future but don't get involved in complications, don't worry, don't be anxious: planning appears to get through but generally doesn't get completely fulfilled. Therefore, live in 'today', enjoy the present moment. The future always remains in the custody of possibilities; then, why to worry?

The human brain supplies uninterrupted energy to desires by the force of which they dance in the mind in colourful garments. Our tendencies are inert in themselves but the mind charges motion in them. All this goes on happening in a natural manner under the flood light of consciousness; however, applying our intense discriminative intelligence we can monitor and ordain these forces of desires.

Tao gave words to the idea in the 6th Century BC:

"*Nature works with stable discipline. She does not exist for a noble king, nor does she stop its work for a wicked king. If we behave with tranquil mind and regulated order then the sun of good luck will dawn, but if we live an in-disciplined, uncontrolled life then the doom becomes a certainty.*"

Where does agitation Germinate?

In the following spheres of darkness agitation germinates:

Immoral sensuous indulgence

Excessive desire for wealth

Anger	Attachment	Lethargy
Cruelty	Atheism	Nescience
Fear of death	Dejection	Fear of holocaust
Fear of total defeat		

Uncertainties of Modern Times

The present time, which we have taken as a boon of science and technology, is laden with several contradictions and conflicts. Such abnormalities create further confusion in our minds – enhancing our *Klesha* (agony):

The sensitive feeling for humanity has been encroached extensively. In place of tenderness of humane sentiments and nicety, mechanical gadgets, computers, T.V., information technology and marketing have filled up the human life.

People seldom talk about the search of truth. The reality of existence is explained away by numerical equations.

Innocence of heart is no more a virtue.

Fantastic absurdity has overshadowed the delicacy of literature. Emotional sensitivity has been chewed up by beastly erotic actions. Criminal instincts are highlighted by imaginary stories.

Fields of art are deserted; our heritage of fine poetry is devastated by corrupt ideas. Where all creation, which touched our core, has gone?

Market-ism and consumerism have swallowed our culture.

The identity of humans is in jeopardy. This stale state has created emptiness in life.

Ideals are almost extinct as is clearly reflected in our system of democracy, even at the highest level.

Question-marks have been pasted upon the Self, the God, and the Absolute Truth.

Fierce hurricane of sensuousness has blasted our character, moral relationships and parameters of fidelity.

Satiation of fantasy remains the only aim of our life: one way or the other!

Science also stumbles at some level of its prospect because of self-contradictory aspects of understanding.

Clemency, love, goodwill, helping attitude – all vanished, except selfish pomp and show.

... And so on ...

What shall we do now? Where do we go from here? Whom should we make our North Pole?

There seems only one way out for us to save overselves from these Tsunamis: to reorganize the ancient wisdom in view of the newer challenges, and to imbibe that into our life.

Mental Agony: Directives of the Gitā

In the above account we get only a glimpse of causes which produce turmoil in our mind. The Gitā tells us in definitive terms, how we can come alive in spite of bashings of the sweeping wind.

क्लैब्यं मा स्म गमः पार्थ नैतत्त्वय्युपपद्यते।
क्षुद्रं हृदयदौर्बल्यं त्यक्त्वोत्तिष्ठ परंतप।।

(2:3)

Yield not to impotence, O Partha! It does not befit thee. Cast off this mean weakness of heart! Stand up, O Parantapa!

When in the battle-field of *Kurukshetra*, Arjuna glanced at the enormous army of Kauravas; the enemy in opposite camp just ready to fight, he became somewhat nervous. It was not because of his cowardice or weaker disposition in anyway, but he could see several of his brethrens, family relations, gurus and friends in formations of the imposing foe; therefore his mind became perturbed; he could foresee death, dejection, defeat and sense of dispossession. Trembling, he put aside his bow-and-arrows and with folded hands bowed before Sri Krishna praying that he did not intend to fight with the near-and-dear ones, even if Kauravas were to take over the kingdom. How were he to kill those whom he adored and worshipped, and those who were close to his bosom?

In this scenario, Sri Krishna who was acting as his charioteer directs him in somewhat 'harsh' words: 'not to behave as a timid person, and to fight with calm and determined mind'.

Many a times, we, the mundane people, also throw away our arms in the battle-field of life, crushingly pressurized by varied fears as well as attachments. Our thoughts vibrate and sway. Weakness clutches our thinking, and impotency bedecks our valour. We abandon our duty, and turn into an earthworm.

The Gitā challenges, even in the most dismal situation one should not leave hope; one must go on striving determinately with courage and full potential. Then only one wins. By doing our duty vigorously, the terror of the problem vanishes.

Sri Krishna further declares

You have grieved for those that should not be grieved for; yet you speak words of wisdom. The wise grieve neither for the living nor for the dead.

(2:11)

The death is immanent, present everywhere; and imminent: sure to happen, and its fear as well as grief about the dear ones also appears to be a natural instinct. But if we could evolve our own philosophy and rational attitude towards life, our sorrows could be minimized. The Gitā radiates such a wisdom which is founded on scientific reasoning. Our Self, or *Ātman*, is integral to the Cosmic Energy. Energy can never be destroyed. Our body is a factor of 'matter' which on apparent 'death' gets converted into the eternal energy, and on another stratum of time-space the 'energy' of life once again changes into 'matter'. The 'matter' as well as the 'energy' can neither be created anew nor destroyed. The balance of equation remains constant; only they mutually swap from one state of existence to the other, i.e., energy to matter and *vice versa*. Then, who dies? What is born? For whom should one lament or why to repent? or why to be afraid and of whom to be afraid?

Going ahead with this reference, Arjuna asks Sri Krishna: even the man does not wish to indulge himself, who instigates him to perform sinful acts?

Sri Krishna Answers:

It is desire, it is anger born of the collecting all sinful. This desire is the foe of man in this world.

(3:37)

Absurd, conflicting desires create passion and attachment for worldly allurements, and when desires remain unfulfilled, anger suddenly erupts. The attachment and the anger both give birth to anxiety and indecision. Then, where remains peace?

धूमेनाव्रियते वन्हिर्यथादर्शो मलेन च।
यथोल्बेनावृतो गर्भस्तथा तेनेदमावृतम्।।

(3:38)

As fire is enveloped by smoke, as mirror by dust, as the foetus by membrane in the womb, so the wisdom is enveloped by desire and anger.

Greed gives birth to strong passion, a hankering for sensuous indulgence and then dissatisfaction. This, however, does not mean that you live in rampant poverty, do not earn prosperity, remain in perpetual want, abhor success and material comforts and ultimately die in deprival. But it surely means that one must not crumble away, like a doll of mud, under the pressure of excessive voracity for possession, gluttony of wealth and meeting the senseless demands of the senses. It is an established fact that beyond the management of our security – comfortable living with solvency to meet requirements of our family – fabulous richness has not much significance; outside of this limit, the abundance of money can't provide additional happiness and peace. Then, why to bring up and nourish the cause of turmoil and disquietude in life?

It is said further –

The senses, the mind and the intellect are said to be its seat; through these, the sensuous desire deludes the man, veiling his wisdom. (3:40)

In this way, by knowing the supreme consciousness, which is subtler than the intellect, and by knowing the mind applying your prudence, O' Mighty Arjuna! You must destroy the desire, lust and passion, which stand as your enemy.

(3:43)

It is an arduous task to control the mind without understanding its structure. Therefore, analyse the root cause of uneasiness of mind and then only restrain and regulate the situation; control the movement of happenings within. Be alert about tricks of the mind! Watch carefully! Let the desire come and dance within but make them seated at their proper place. Not by force, but by cleverness you can do it.

The causal factor of all tidal waves in the mind is 'duality' – *Dwanda*, a conflicting pair of two opposites.

इच्छाद्वेषसमुत्थेन द्वन्द्वमोहेन भारत।
सर्वभूतानि संमोहं सर्गे यान्ति परंतप।।

(7:27)

By the delusion of conflicts arising from desire and aversion, O Bharata! all beings are subjected to delusion at birth, O Parantapa!

The desire, or yearning, means, attraction, longing, charm. Aversion means hatred, repulsion, disgust. Liking and disliking, or attraction and rebuff create happiness and unhappiness. These are dualities – always together but engaged in clashing with each other! Hot-cold, pleasure-pain, profit-loss, life-death, fame-infamy, light-darkness, honour-dishonour, and several other such pairs! Because of these conflicting factors, our mind becomes exalted at one moment and depressed at the other. It ascends sometimes, on the ninth cloud, sometimes lies low in the bottomless ditch. But even while living amidst the struggles if we could maintain a critical balance by our discriminative intellect, the sting of depression becomes ineffective.

Balance is the key to happiness; Come, what may! If we are convinced that 'this will also go away', the odd situation also smoothens considerably. Face the rough sector of journey, change pathway, search for fresh alternatives – but don't lose courage. Don't remain stuck-up in stupidity – 'This is the end of the world'. Hard work, perseverance, vigilance, faith and justified distancing from the clutter may keep you delighted: no other treasure or luxury of the world can keep you in permanent state of happiness, ecstasy, or the feeling of overwhelming joy; only the enlightenment and cognizance of the Self can do that.

In the modern context, people, mostly, convolute in the pursuit of filthy activities which are mostly futile from the point of view of obtaining health and peace. In the end, the runner gets exhausted and thinks that although his achievements were fabulous, a deep void reigns within him.

The Gitā Announces

मोघाशा मोघकर्माणो मोघज्ञाना विचेतसः।
राक्षसीमासुरीं चैव प्रकृतिं मोहिनीं श्रिताः।।

(9:12)

Of vain hopes, of vain actions, of vain knowledge, and senseless they verily are possessed of delusive nature of diabolic.

Without performing action, involving in day-dreaming, that 'a miracle will take place someday; we will get freedom from *Klesha* of un-conducive situations, and enter the realm of pleasure and peace, then our mind will be rewarded with equanimity' – this thought is a foolishness of the first order in which we go on revolving, day-in and day-out.

However, it is desirable to be hopeful about the future, but without an input of action, a flight of fantasy throws you into a whirl of confusion. In the same manner, to go on doing hard labour without any substantial consequence, or to accumulate ignorance taking it for wisdom of high order, generates pain, emptiness and disconcert: all mixed up in the mind. These three states: inaction, futile action and ignorance; are the source of sufferance and irritation. The Gitā helps us by showing a path to escape these tragedies.

If we live in simplicity by way of natural system – without hypocrisy, without simulation of superficial virtues or goodness, then negative tendencies can't enter our psyche. But, regretfully, we adopt valueless purpose as the aim of our life, and in the end we fail miserably.

The Sources of Pitiable and Painful Conditions in Life

Agitation, intensive emotional fit, unending hedonism, improbable ambition, passion for comfort and fabulous luxury, thirst to achieve popularity by dirty means, and on, are the sources that make our life painful and pitiable. In contrast, a life of equilibrium, middle path, and righteous ways to achieve the aforesaid bonanza could be considered as progressive. Beware! The pull of intemperance is very strong; it may drag you, allure you, towards a path full of stinking sludge.

So, keep away from the mad rat-race. The peace of mind could be achieved by autonomous living, self-sufficient support, indifference towards futility of charming things outside in the world, self-reliance, and by earning money for a smooth run.

Follow the path of happiness; keep the pain at bay by management, and Oneness with the Creator as the Creator does not need anything; therefore, there remains a minimal requirement for the person who is connected with the Creator.

The teachings of Gitā are not sermons, rather directives for practical living. A prime quality-life is a melodious symphony: reasonable, productive and invaluable. To achieve this target, we have to get out of 'uncertainties of modern time' as enlisted above, to cast-off our imperfections and inferiority. Be courageous! Diagnose the truth of life and death; manage sensuality, anger, greed, hatred, etc. And survive the bashing of inner Tsunami which erupts in mind at times; by insight cognition of ignorance, structure of conflicts in the duality of worldly systems, and irrelevance of useless activities which we are mostly engaged in.

This is the enlightenment, the cosmic learning of the Gitā by following which one can escape from the assault and aggressiveness of Tsunami syndrome in our being.

Road Signals in Gitā,
Balance in thinking-pattern,
Mental poise in uncertain situations,
Simplicity in life,
Freedom from immoral gratification,
Analysis of ignorance,
Recognition of worthlessness in gluttony,
Protection from mental fluttering,
Knowing the source of discontent,
Security from storm of modernity,
Mantra of – our life, our responsibility,

Select the pearl carefully! Beware of the hidden agenda of the mind. Stick to your own principles and values. Contemplate on the eternal truth. Don't make the satiation of desires the only aim of your life – there could be even higher objectives of our coming on this planet. Hence:

Break away the cage, and fly across the sky of freedom!

•

Symphony – 1

Circles within Circles

'To control the thought-waves of mind is 'Yoga'. By this technique, the seeker gets the self established in his own natural state of existence; else, when he is not in the state of Yoga – or of meditation, he remains just like his thought-waves, *(Chitta Vritti),* which are of five types; some painful, others non-painful; these are :

Right Knowledge – Direct perception, inferred knowledge, learning from scriptures.

Wrong Knowledge – It is not the true knowing, which is not based on the real nature of things.

Verbal delusion – It arises when words do not correspond to reality.

Sleep – This is a wave of thought about nothingness. It has no base to exist on.

Memory - In this state, perceived objects are not forgotten but come back off and on to consciousness.

According to **Patanjali**:

"These waves of mind could be controlled by means of practice and non-attachment".

What could be a simpler and more perfect description of mental tendencies than this? If we throw a pebble into a clean, tranquil, small lake, we create circular wave-rings, one after another, softly moving and spreading across the area. If we continue to throw pebbles one after the other at short intervals, then these circles of waves go on rising and ultimately forming a confused pattern! Our mind behaves exactly in the same pattern; these circles represent our desires, tendencies *(Vritti),* passions, temptations and coveting. Circles within circles, desires within desires; we, in the end, can't locate the centre and the peripheries of such circular waves. They don't have any definite locations, are restless and always on the move.

The desires for worldly objects are uninterruptedly shot by our sense organs into the lake of over mind, producing whirls of agitated cravings to possess. These wheels of fantasy create our personal world – such a world which is generally different from that of the other people. These are our special 'hells'! And individual 'heavens'!!

Our holistic personality is constituted by four elements, or factors: body, mind, intellect and ego. Our consciousness, or *Atma-tatva*, illumines the activities of these elements; or, sometimes it is covered by the ego which, in fact remains hidden, and even our intellect cannot know it. Under such circumstances we get confused and deluded, our thoughts toss and tumble and our life sticks up in chaos; we forget our innate nature – that is, our pristine Self (Consciousness or *Ātman*). And we perpetually become happy and unhappy!

Our elemental consciousness factor represents the integral radiance of omnipresent energy of the Creator (Cosmic Intelligence, Cosmic Power, Absolute *Brahman*). Mind, intellect and ego constitute our psyche, or *Chitta*. A blend of ego, instinct, inclination, tendency, aptitude, etc., guides our journey of life. Our ego plays sometimes with our intelligence and at the other time with our mind. Western psychologists opine that the ego, or the self, is the same aspect of the personality. According to the Indian philosophy, the self (ego) and the consciousness *(Self, Ātman)* are two different powers, but could be unified into one by the efforts of the seeker. That means – by enlightened knowledge the ego could be annihilated which ultimately merges into the *Ātman*.

Our mind could be harder than a rock or more sensitive than a 'touch-me-not' sapling. One can see such tenderness in the relationships of love and hate. At times one does not hesitate even to sacrifice one's life, but at the moment of a crisis of faith, the intimacy shatters off. Thus, goes on the drama of instincts and weaknesses of our mind.

Beside this, the mind, or even our psyche, could be fragmented by the impact of profit or loss, life or death, fame or infamy – particularly by the negative part of these pairs.

In this regard, I remember an incidence. There lived a man – barber by profession, in our village. People called him Ramji although his name was Ram Gopal. Ramji was a custodian of charming personality, always smiling, laced with humility and good manners. He possessed some agricultural land. He was financially self-sufficient. At the age of about 50, Ramji was elected as the leader of his clan in the area; now happier and more fulfilled.

But, the wheel of fame turned the other way. Once, on some matter of contention, people of his caste became against him. He was criticized, insulted and made to leave the societal lunch. Only a few of his close relatives supported him; rest of the gathering was against his view.

For some days, he showed a nervous break-down, not talking to anybody, not doing anything, morose and blank. Then he was struck by madness – and within two years he died.

This is the hard hammer of infamy on the head. Sensitivity of mind! Voodoo effect! Crumbling of the ego!

Our *Ātman* always remains unstained, colourless, changeless, and unaffected by happenings in our psyche or *chitta*, but at times, multicoloured, vibrant forms and figures appear to dance, shadowing the bright light of *Ātman*; it happens as manifestation of desires through the medium of ego. This is the root cause of our suffering and sorrow.

Mind and the Brain

To understand the mind, we have to know some aspects of the brain. The physical brain of humans is more complex and highly evolved than that of other animals. Our sense organs continuously relay stimuli to the neuro-chemical system of brain to excite the whole structure. The volume of our brain is about 1370 cubic centimetre, containing more than hundred billion neurons (the specialized nerve cells); each neuron is connected with about 10 thousand other neurons which transmit messages in a flow – like incessant sparking of electric current. This data goes on storing in the memory chamber – of course, to be sorted out subsequently. This activity takes place in the melee of chemical messengers through the nerve threads.

How do awareness, thoughts, emotions and instincts originate in the physical brain? The subject remains a mystery although much time and money are invested to support the research in this area:

Our thoughts stimulate the network of nervous system and dendrons (fine fibers branched as micro-twigs, at the end of a nerve-cell).

On the branch-ends of this Dendron, units of 'mind' are clustered, which are called *psychos*.

These psychos in totality form our mind, or *mānas*, which functions in the realm of the Self or Consciousness.

The psychos survive the human death in the form of psycho energy which consists of, or encloses within, our memories of unfulfilled desires, aptitude, tendencies and instincts.

The soul, spirit or consciousness is beyond the periphery of scientific investigation because science happens within the gamut of 'ego', while consciousness is a field of trans-ego.

Between the human mind and the *Ātman*, there exists a unique and original relationship. Although we experience and vaguely feel that our existence revolves around a nucleus of energy centre, or core, called as *Ātman* (Soul, Sublimed Self), yet we do not have a clear cognizance of this kernel or nave of our own.

Brain is a physical ephemeral entity, but mind is impersonal – without shape, size or attributes. It takes birth from the stimuli generated by the objects of the world which are accumulated and processed by our brain. It has been concluded by mystics as well as atomic physicists that the world of objects is nothing but a product of our mind. It is "nothingness" or "*Māyā* " as they call it.

It could be deciphered by scientific research that humans possess freedom to work according to free-will; the centre of such instinct lies deep inside the brain.

The World as Experience Only

The world is only an experience: claims **Ancient Zen philosophy** and further clarifies,

"The heaven and earth could be separated only by a minuscule distance. If you want to know the ultimate Truth, don't care about 'right' or 'wrong' because a battle between right and wrong is the main disease of our mind."

The existential world is an experience of provocation generated by our senses. Such a world is structured on the foundation of our knowledge and thoughts which are framed inside the brain and transmitted further to create our mind.

The objects and happenings in the world are neither 'good' nor 'bad' in themselves – they are as they must be, but when our senses come in contact with them, then sensation, or perception develops. On the basis of experience of these sensory reactions we go on creating our private world. Every person experiences differently about the same thing; this is the greatest wonder! Thus, everybody has his own world – not matching with that of the others!

Such enormous power, force, or energy which synthesizes our external experiences and goes on painting our world anew, is beyond our capacity to analyze. In other words, we cannot say what these forces are; hence we can never perceive the real nature of the world! So, what can we do? Shall we stop our thoughts? This is an improbable task. Those who boast that their thoughts are under their control are generally hypocrites. However, one can 'see' the flow of one's thoughts by the technique of meditation, Zen, Tao, *Dhyān* and deep contemplation – that is, we can practise to search the source of thoughts. By vigorous practice and concentration this attainment could be possible to a certain extent, but even then at the time of some weaker moment, any of the wild and corrupt thoughts can create agitation, and this is not possible to predict!

What shall we do with our perceptions and reactions to events which uphold the making and unmaking of our world? Our world is nothing more than our own imagination or apparent sensation – which we may name as experience. Define this phenomenon in as many disordered way as you like but the fact remains unaltered,

Yet, how to get along?

The great philosopher Samuel Kant has shown us a way by walking on which, perhaps, we may be able to rearrange our thoughts, and hence our world, in a somewhat sensible manner.

Let us see:

We must continuously arrange our thoughts in a suitable way – not in a kaleidoscopic pattern but in conformity with the time and space in which we find ourselves. Do not make only an imaginary picture rather draw a classified, well-organized map so that the ever-changing incoming data could be controlled properly.

It means – the vibrant, riotous colours of in pouring stimuli go on changing incessantly, and if we do not classify them then stable scenery cannot be made out of them.

The underlying meaning of Kant indicates that if keeping the need of time and place in mind we learn to utilize our experience in a right manner, then even the fluctuating arrangements of the world cannot make us miserable. The point is – not to amalgamate our encounters with sensuality and not to leave any opportunity to use for enhancing knowledge to our advantage.

There are two types of persons in the world: *Idealists*, who always remain in their own world which they themselves frame in their mind; their world stands on the crutches of fantasy, own thoughts and self-screwed diagnoses of things and events. Second category of people includes *Realists* who accept the 'concreteness' of the world and face the life squarely. Such a person remains ready to deal with hard truths of life, believes in them, and assesses ever-changing situation with practicality; his decisions are free from sentiments and emotions. It means: the realist does not live in idealist's utopia, being in front to confront with problems.

In spite of such classification, it is seen that one can neither be a purely idealist nor realist in totality. A balanced admixture of both attitudes is desirable because pure realistic approach towards the world results into a mechanical living; no pathway for evolution of humanitarian niceties, love or tenderness. Moreover, in hard-rock realism there exists always a chance of getting lost in the mire of materialism, inside of *Chakras,* circles-within-circles of tangled thoughts. Therefore, the 'middle path' of Buddha could make a golden rule – as ever!

What Dose Gitā Say about 'Mind'?

We may be high degree influential and powerful, we could have been victorious in innumerable, seemingly invincible situations of life, and every problem had appeared to us as a cake-walk, yet sometimes our psyche becomes weak and fragile. We lose courage!

In the battle-field of *Kurukshetra*, Arjuna was engulfed by somewhat similar mental weakness. Understanding his emotional condition, Lord Krishna told him in harsh tone, "*Don't be a victim of impotency; it is not for the bravest of all warriors like you*". This was a method of instigation, or inspiration, which Sri Krishna adopted. A challenge! A rejection! We know, at the time of an open challenge our mind becomes alert and ready to face any eventuality. This means, we rearrange our reactions and experiences in view of a new situation at a given time and place.

In the Gitā, a practical philosophy has been put forth. If a philosophy remains only theoretical, it can hardly do any good to the humanity therefore it must also be a utilitarian concept useful for a purpose. But, at the same time, it is generally difficult to make the philosophy a tool for practical living. Although we formulate several moral and ethical policies by proposing lofty theories, it is usually not easy to make their use on the revolving stage of life. For example –truth, non-violence, self-control, non-attachment, contentment, non-jealousy, love, equanimity, etc., make a lengthy list, which are discussed as sermons by every religion. The Gitā also narrates repeatedly the glory of these virtues. But is it easy to follow, in words and spirit, these saintly worthy arduous paths? Perhaps one in million could do it! Obviously because of this fact, despite a continual flow of such pristine teachings, the vagaries of the world have not lessened – rather they have increased! One can definitely be better and superior by trying and imbibing and following these teachings.

Why is it So?

Because the real meaning of the ancient wisdom has not been explained properly; even, at times, in order to meet their personal motives the selfish elements of the society have misled the laymen. Consequently, plain and innocent people were sucked-up in rituals, fanaticism, desires of heaven, terror of hell and decay of self-confidence. In the glittering greed for luxury and power, the custodians of religion themselves became corrupt. Teachings of such 'gurus' fired back. 'Non-passion for prosperity' was defined erroneously, and we were wedded to beggary. In absolute poverty! A rampant weakness crept into our being; inactivity prevailed. We left everything to fate or destiny. We were fragmented into caste and social hierarchy. We were enslaved for centuries!

By common sense, an intelligent person can find the real substance of religious teachings so that the utility of this wisdom and its applicability, relevance and moral rectitude, uprightness or correct and honest way could be comprehended. This very knowledge may lead to the realization of the Absolute Truth; the Gitā is an inexhaustible stream of such wisdom that leads one to purity, revelation and enlightenment.

The following are some aspects of this wisdom:

Desire means foolish longings of self-indulgence which could be painful to others. One must avoid irrelevant craze for gratification of senses, and material gluttony.

Redundant luxuriance includes those materials or acquirements which are extraneous to our safety cover.

Sensuality – Sensuality is immoral, against the societal laws, breaching the pious relationships in the family and inviting contempt of natural law of being. It is a corrupt passion.

Mind is the foundation of our life; it can't be fully controlled but it could be trained for integrity.

There exist **pairs of contradicting elements** *(Dwanda)* in every walk of life; it is the law of Nature, e.g. happiness–unhappiness, hot–cold, etc. One must keep a critical balance by applying one's real wit and acumen.

Intensive expectation for the fruits of action: Make the fruition your target but it is a folly to be over-worried, to lose calm of life and to tremble in imbalance in high hope of reward. The fruits of our present actions ripe in the future; leave them at the altar of the Lord. Else you will disintegrate and crumble!

Truth – Ensuring our own survival, and viewing the time, place and laws of the land, it is desirable that we follow the fundamentals of truthfulness and honesty. Such a practice generates peace and power in our being.

Non-violence–Don't hurt any being – physically, emotionally or mentally; it all comes under violence. But non-violence must not be considered as timidity or fragility; it should be expressed as a powerful means at the time of a challenge to protect the self, our own country and the weak. Non-violence in not cowardice.

Contentment – One must work hard with a well-planned method to make progress and earn prosperity, but at the same time there should not be any instability of mind and madness about excessive material gains.

Non-hatred – As for as possible keep away from jealousy, hate, enmity and resentment. If this practice appears to be difficult, then in such a situation be indifferent, non-attached or clear-headed.

Love – The Absolute Cosmic Energy dwells within you as well as in other existence. By knowing this, try to keep positive relationship with all.

Equanimity – Don't be upset at the time of crisis; come out of severe conflict–as soon as possible, and don't get intoxicated by great achievements. Balance is the key to happiness.

At the Depth of Mind

Arya dev, a great saint of Budhism opines: Two things are necessary to bring stability at the depth of our mind, 1. Temperance (innocence, restraint, purity) of mind which can be achieved by enlightened non-attachment with the material world and by minimizing the sensual desire for satisfying the bodily lust; 2. Serenity of the mind could be attained by analyzing the causal factors of *Klesha* (pain, agony, sorrow), and subsequently by removing such causes. Balance of mind and calmness play a major role in getting un-quivering peace.

For achievement of these two states, practice of meditation and contemplation upon one's ideal *(Ishta devtā)* is mandatory.

During intensive meditation, or *Dhyāna,* we can scan the weaving of our thoughts, and check them from falling in indulgence. By concentrating upon the highest object of our being – the Absolute Almighty, in the form of our inclination – our mind and our psyche get a foothold, a support, and thence our life-energy does not astray in de-meritorious directions. Unscrupulous forces of passion, anger, desires and other negativities cannot be crushed and annihilated but at least they could be subdued, tamed, made gentler and less intense, by smart management and persēverance. If we determine and consciously follow the process of discipline meticulously, the black hurricane of our thoughts will subside in course of time. The basic cognitive faculty lies in the fact that an intelligent person makes out the nature of his own mind by scanning the fibers of his thought, yet he does not suppress the mind. Suppression is not probable and also not desirable. The enlightened sage, thus, after dissecting his own thought-flow, wanders in the world and does his duty, allocated by *karma*, through his innocent intuition. No tsunami, or conflicts or contradictions, can ever turn such a renunciation into a sorrowful worm.

By soft and mild efforts, divert the mind away from the objects which generally create turmoil; then usher it into the subtler aspects of life – like, love, empathy, serenity, eternal truth, and so on.

At the finer level of our existence, the brilliance of the Absolute radiates which fills our intellect with the light of immaculate knowledge, or *Prajnā;* and, thus, our mind is blessed with the ecstasy of eternal peace.

The customary knowledge, in ordinary sense of data, information or stimuli which our senses accumulate as experiences, is no doubt essential for our survival and worldly affairs, but intrinsically it remains unfulfilling and disappointing – just like the life which remains engulfed in carnality and debauchery; no one can ever realize the Truth by walking on the path of vortex and temptation.

Therefore, fly beyond the senses and their fields, enter the Reality and merge with transcendental 'One'. Thereafter wander in the 'Nothingness' which fills the region beyond the periphery of mind. This Truth reigns further and yonder the deepest layers of mind, away from its extension, dimensions and reach.

Transformation of Mind

If we could alter the nature of our thought-pattern, no upheavals of tsunami within can make us unhappy. But we have to work hard for making such aim a reality. First of all, we have to understand the relationship between 'reasons' 'emotions' and desires or stimuli created by our 'senses'. The 'reasons' or relational awareness could be recognized by discriminative intellect, or *Viveka;* emotions are the waves arising from the ego and dancing on the past experiences of the *person;* and desires germinate on the complex substratum of unconsciousness. All these three factors – reasons, emotions and desires, evermore circle within the grooves of mind-intellect-ego trio. A harmonized balance of mutual coordination amongst these factors could be achieved only by *Viveka* – the purified, intense intellect; *Viveka* can rip-open the absurdity of our psyche and expose the unsoiled Truth from within.

Our mind should be trained in such a way that even if any 'person', 'thing' or 'situation' is separated or parted away from us, such an event should not drown us in extreme pain or a sense of total loss. The mind should, at such a time of crisis, try to get out of the swamp of sorrow, as early as possible, and let go the flow of events. Just watch!

One must keep a relationship of indifference and renunciation with penchant and craving for things – not involving in bondage or slavery. Then only it may become possible to witness the trail of pleasant as well as unpleasant incidences and to face every situation with calm and tranquil mind – without being unnerved.

The highway of true knowledge opens the vistas for our crescendo, if we could take cognizance of our own shortcomings and negativities. People used to say about Socrates that in the whole of Athens, he was the wisest person because it was he "*who knew that he did not know anything*".

We, in ignorance, keep busy in the search of true knowledge and blissful happiness, but we do not realize that the senses are inert and nescient in themselves.

This is our psyche *(Chitta)* which can usher us into the path of light, with a condition, of course, that we have to make the *mānas* a balanced friend. In case we could rightly train our mind, under the illumination of our *Ātman*, or spirit, then all that which lies beyond the reach of senses may come to our fore. This is 'That' Truth.

Adapt to newer pathways in life; let faith and conviction be sprouted in the being. In the beginning, the new path may appear strange and uncertain but slowly, by practice, the same will become certain, well-defined and safe. Test it by doing it yourself!

•

Resonance – 1

My world and your world –
are not the same,
Our *awareness* – is our life,
O'mind! 'flickering' thy name!

Thoughts – quivering …
All is uncertain!
Yet, taming of mind
may lessen our pain

The past is dead,
Future yet to born,
Laugh in the Now!
Time flows on and on …

What will be … will be …
Stream of flow; block can none,
All is probable! Yet it's –
Your freedom to choose one

Universe – born of void …
Atom is a 'nothingness' too,
My body, a cluster of particles,
Time, space, moment – all voodoo

You are free to act –
Leave the worry of fruition,
Death is the time of Freedom –
If you detach from passion

Control the mind by *Viveka,*
By mind check the ego amiss,
Get plugged to Cosmic Divine –
He blesses with shining bliss!

In the Kingdom of consciousness –
Reason becomes dull and tame,
Bounded by the Time-space,
Trembles the logic mundane

God is with a shape and form,
And as abstract, too,
Swapping from one to the other –
As particles and energy waves do!

This is your own life, and so –
Find your own yonder way,
You are responsible for the deeds,
No one would share sins; I pray!

•

Take in a Stride – 1

Study main Scriptures of all main religions of the world.

Get out of narrow-minded setup.

Search the stress-nodes of thought and behavior, and untie the knots.

Life is not an eternal bed of roses; remain ready to bear the thorns alike: with a smile, of course.

Restrain, to-day, passion for comfort and luxury by practising temperance; you know nothing about tomorrow.

Future remains always in veil, hence continue to solve the problems of today; definitely today.

Begin to live on one value of an ideal life, *Dharma*, as put forth by our scriptures. The rest will follow.

If you watch intently the waves of your own mind, they start subsiding.

Write down, in a classified manner, all your major experiences of life – e.g., friendship, lack of fulfillment, success, love, hatred, etc. Read them after a gap of a few years.

By following the given exercises, the structure and organization your world will be projected out and the road map of your journey will be high-lighted. Amend them wherever and whenever necessary.

Dimensions of Unhappiness

After many years of intensive ascetic life, one day Gautam experienced that a total alteration was taking place in his consciousness: a deep-rooted change in personality. He sat under a *peepal (Ficus religiosa)* tree meditating, with a vow not to get up till he got enlightenment. For six days and nights in a row, he remained in that posture concentrating on his own Awareness. On the rise of the 7th morning star, suddenly he received the grace of the Light: an original knowledge of the Cosmic Power. That was the manifestation of unlimited awareness in entirety. The bondage of illusion was broken away. And Gautam was transformed into Buddha, the Buddha!

After the enlightenment, Buddha addressed his five fellow sages who had lived with him earlier. Buddha taught them the right religion and narrated about various dimensions and intensity of 'sorrows' *(Dukha)*.

There is no suitable English synonym for *Dukha* which could illustrate the exact import of pain or agony in totality. Yet we may comprehend by a regimen of several words: suffering, dejection, agony, passion, angst, undesirable company, separation from the loved ones, etc. *Dukha* is the severest disease in the world. Although the world is not filled up to the brim by pain and misery, yet their multiple worry, forceful desires, hopelessness, frustration, depression – torture our mind, off and on.

In this regard, Buddha has laid down four *Ārya Satya* (Eternal Truths) or Noble Truths:

Sufferings do exist

Formation of sufferings

Extinction of sufferings

Path to the extinction of sufferings

Pain and misery (sorrows) are existent – birth, old age, disease, death, grief, hatred pain and aches. More intense is the pain of separation from near-and-dear ones, and union with malicious.

Root Cause of Suffering

The main cause of sorrow is ignorance, *Agyān*; lack of comprehension of the Truth. We take the worldly affairs for granted, as immutable. We go on convoluting in the wistful day-dream, resentment, jealousy, anxiousness, etc., which are the outcome of our sensual indulgence. Such negativities of life take birth because all the time we are busy in collecting the luxuriant pleasure, trying to keep them safe and secured, and always afraid of losing our 'kingdom of happiness'. Excessive passion, desire and involvement in redundancy are the basic causal factors of unhappiness.

How sorrows, pains and sufferance could be annihilated? It could be, if we realize the innate nature of life. Uncontaminated beauty of life in raw! By cognizance of the Reality! What is the original nature of 'things'? How far they continue to exist? If we could read this easily and comprehend the truth behind all such things and happenings of the world, we will be less sorrowful. This wisdom when arises in our being, peace and bliss prevail in the life.

What is the technique for weeding out pains and sorrows? According to Mahatma Buddha, only by living in rhythm with the Law of Being – i.e., *Dharma,* the sorrows can be removed. And this *Dharma* is a total Awareness: in knowledge, thoughts, speech, actions, efforts; to achieve wholeness in being alert and remaining concentrated. In other words, one must be in a state of complete awareness towards one's thoughts, speech and actions existing in an equipoise life- style and the Truth so that the agony does not sprout.

In varied walks of life, factors of non-comprehension and queerness of mind are present in a mixed way; this must be meticulously analysed as well as understood, else we will always invite weariness and annoyance. The negativity of things or happenings has to be scanned out at the first look. To know ignorance is the major victory for achieving true knowledge.

Meaning of Our Life

What is the meaning of our life? What is its ultimate aim? Such questions do not appear to be logical. If we could see through the whole existence, and also that we are a part of that power which created the universe, then there remains no necessity to search for the purpose of our life. The Universe 'is'; we 'are' in that; whatever is, it is that. This is a subject of exalted realization; it is transcendental; it is a vibrant experience of dissolution. It can't be answered in words. If we alter our awareness, then all the queries could be answered. The purpose of our life is embedded in the purpose of the universe.

Ignorance is the mother of dejection and discontent. Education annihilates ignorance; not general or ordinary education, which is mostly information but that of life and Nature which could open gates of wisdom, give insight into existence, discriminative intellect and sublimed layer of life itself. What we are not? Who we are not? Meditate on such unusual questions; the sting of sorrow will give lesser pain. Is our existence illusion, a deception, an artifice or a fallacy? Do we attach undue importance to senseless events, more than what they deserve? Am I only a 'body' whose numerous circles are moving speedily towards death? If yes, then why sorrow, pain, and anguish? Why do we remain sunken in the sludge of sufferings? If stricken by harsh time and grief; and want to cry, then cry, weep, lament; but get out of the mire, as early as possible. Try and break away!

Is it difficult? Yes, it is! But if one keeps balanced attitude and equipoise towards life, and a sharp discriminatory mind set, then it becomes less difficult.

A young boy, the only son of an old woman, died. He was her life support and love. The husband of this woman had passed away long back. She was devastated by grief and agony. On the same day, Buddha visited her house. The lady questioned Buddha, "Why has such a tragedy and curse befallen upon me? Can you bring this dead son of mine to life?" Buddha replied calmly: "Mother! Please bring one fistful of rice from any house, in this village, where no one has died so far; then only I shall answer your question, and give life back to your son". The old lady went from house to house: if nobody had died there so far. But, alas! She could not find such a house. She returned to her own dwelling where the sage was sitting. She told him that there was no house where death had not visited.

Buddha said "Mother! Now you got the answer of your questions: "The world moves within the 'Wheel of time' (Kāl Chakra). Every creature has to whirl according to karma; the cycle of birth and death goes on incessantly for the mortal beings until the individual exhausts the bondage of karma. Your pain is unbearable, no doubt, but it is urgent to come out of this heartache. Have courage! Think about the Creator, and be composed".

After listening to the enlightening words the old women was heartened and her suffering was lessened a lot. She became his follower.

One must keep in mind that the world is a delusion, an illusion. Its real nature is not that which we see or experience. It is unstable, not stable; it is mortal, not immortal; it is finite, not infinite. It is *Māyā*!

Māyā (illusion) does not mean here that the world is not a reality, an actuality or a perceptible phenomenon. *Māyā* could be understood, too, as our own ignorance existing within the infinite circle of Cosmic Illusion (*Mahā Māyā*). The world appears to be real but our ways of looking at it and of interpreting the happenings are so much distorted that our individual world transforms into a mirage. Such a deceptive, hallucinating world which we erect on the basis of our own wavering experiences and perceptions ultimately collapses within itself, and we anguish from dejection.

Actually, we do not possess an insight about the reality of the world; in its place we build our own world within the rainbow dimensions of our thoughts, which ultimately prove to be a corruption of colours: nothing else!

The awakened man; living in abundant brilliance of awareness, ken and cognizance, is never terrified by the fear of death because he knows that the death is definite: immanent, and nothing could be destroyed through bodily demise as is evident from energy, matter constant. Only our life factor gets transformed to manifest at another plane of time-space. According to atomic physics, the matter changes into energy, and at a suitable time, the energy re-converts into matter. But the equation remains consistent: nothing is lost, nothing is gained! This is the physical truth of the universe.

Then, from where does the horror of non-existence or nothingness come? The most amusing fact is that, till we exist the death will not be there and when it comes, we shall not be there. Why, then, tremble in angst? Therefore, by developing thinking and by following positive philosophy, we could conquer the panic and phobia of our oblivion, a major suffering. And all the mania related to our extinction will be over.

The enlightened person always experiences a loving relationship with his whole life; in other words, he sees the same energy in all beings, and all beings within one power. Having developed this ken, such an evolved person can never nurture antipathy and hatred against any one; the wise of this category keeps him-self away from violence. Just think! With one effort, i.e., by mustering fearlessness and courage, innumerable causes of unhappiness get eradicated! The achiever of such wisdom starts behaving open-heartedly, without contravention, in his actions or thoughts. He does not store the poison of jealousy in his heart. Beside all these achievements, he becomes dexterous, intelligent and judicious in his day-to-day mundane activities. Obviously just by making one consistent effort, one can enter the realm of knowledge, the Truth.

In contrast to this situation, a person with mediocre thoughts remains variously divided; that means, he develops no individuality of his own; he is not a unified personality. His mind remains busy in futile hopping and jumping. But, as we all know, it is necessary to be intensely concentrated if we desire to understand the basic factor of a vibrant life: "what am

I feeling now?" One must breathe within the exquisite awareness to catch hold of the answer to this question!

Swami Vivekanand said (in Vedānt, Voice of Freedom:

We constantly complain that we have no control over our actions, over our thoughts. But how can we have it? If we can get control over the fine movements, if we can get hold of thought at the root, before it has become thought, before it has become action, then it would be possible for us to control the whole... He who knows and controls his own mind knows the secret of every mind and has power over every mind.

Ordinarily, the antonym of 'suffering' is understood to be 'happiness'; we take it for granted that 'happiness' lies in redundant satiation and quenching for the ego through desire fulfillment, but by adopting these methods to catch hold of permanent 'happiness', we can never change the level of our bliss and mental beatitude. It is so because all these techniques are instinct-based, desire-oriented, which are the product of our mind. And the mind changes every second! It is never at rest and at no time satisfied. Clear as it is, by way of sensual satisfaction we can never possess a real 'happiness' because peace, tranquility and virtues can never be cultivated by means of negativity.

We want to survive the sorrows. For such a high goal of life it is desirable to evolve creative traits of mind: self-confidence, optimism, truthfulness, firmness in character, cooperation, empathy, benevolence and goodness. Such emotional structures support us at the time of crisis.

While living within great prosperity, we starve because of a lack of spirituality. Despite this situation, we could be connected with the Almighty by way of pure knowledge which absolves us from sufferance.

We always search momentary 'pleasure' and excitement but we do not know that the acts of kindness and helping the destitute are more satisfactory, peace-giving and stable source of happiness.

All the treatises of wisdom, world over, recognize the following six basic virtues for mankind. These are more or less similar in all the cultures and traditions:

Innocent thoughts and cognizance

Patience and courage

Love and humanity

Integrity in action

Sacrifice of selfishness

Spirituality

These are our personal powers, strength and support. In related aspects, they can be extended and enlarged into several orders of magnitude: enthusiasm for discovering the nature, inquisition to enhance self-knowledge, absence of intolerance, originality in thoughts and actions, practical wisdom, judgment founded on experience, etc.

Select benedictory elements. Absorb the beatitude of life in your being. Practise amnesty and forgiveness. Be tenacious at the time of adversity.

Live your life amusingly. There is hardly anything in the world for which one should diminish one's happiness and peace, yet if ill-luck strikes in personal life, one has to try to come out of the agony as early as possible.

Gitā: The Cosmic Space of Clear Thinking

Even before the war of *Mahabharata* began, Arjuna was mentally gripped by guilty conscience and self torture visualizing the forthcoming holocaust by way of armed conflict. On this, Sri Krishna said – *'You are lamenting for those over whom you are not supposed to mourn, and at the same time you are talking like a highly learned person'.*

Sri Krishna narrates further – 'In the past there was no time when you were not there, I was not there, or these warriors were absent; neither in the future we all will ever be absent'. In other words, 'all are present at all the time' – i.e., the eternal energy (or *Ātma Tatva*), which resides in all beings, is immortal; it is not destroyed by the death of the body.

Then, what is the justification of weeping over losses or separations?

Krishna puts forth that the death is a 'boundary line of a change-over' – it is not the terminal station for life.

देहिनोऽस्मिन यथा देहे कौमारं यौवनं जरा।
तथा देहान्तः प्राप्तिः धीरः तत्र न मुह्यति।।

(2:13)

Just as in this body the soul passes into childhood, youth and old age, so also does he pass into another body; the firm man does not grieve for it.

The *Jeevātma* (soul) after the dropping off of the body manifests at another stratum of time-space. We know that after our childhood and adolescence we enter the state of youth, and then from youth into the old age. At the borders of all these stages, metamorphic changes do occur – in body, mind, thoughts, intellect, etc. – but the *Ātman* remains unchanged all-through. In this very way, the so-called 'death' is also an entry line for forward journey on to a new zone of expression for the Self. It is a transitional phase: then, why to agonize?

In this context, it has been further said : the persons who do not disturb their own equipoise at the time of pleasant or unpleasant happenings, who do not get deranged and crumbled by the sensuous storms and cyclones of desires, they easily achieve *Nirvāna, Moksha* or Freedom!

We must have vital awareness that *Ātman* is immortal, timeless, ageless as well as omnipresent. No one can ever annihilate *Ātman*. It is the Truth.

Then, why the fear of death?

वासांसि जीर्णानि यथा विहाय
नवीन गृहणाति नरोऽपराणि।
तथा शरीराणि विहाय जीर्णा-
न्यन्यानि संयाति नवानि देही।।

(2:22)

Just as a man casts off his worn out clothes and puts on new ones, so also the Self casts off the worn out bodies and enters other new bodies.

And, still beyond this –

Weapons pierce it not, fire burns it not, water wets it not, and wind dries it not.

Therefore, the passing-away of the body is not a matter of terror, anxiety and anguish.

One must comprehend deeper meaning and scientific facts about the aforesaid aspects of life and death. The cosmic energy can never be destroyed. The matter also cannot be done away with: it only alters its form and converts into energy. All particles of matter in our body get dispersed in the space and become energy waves. But even then, in the whole cosmos, the totality of matter-energy equation remains constant. The energy symbolizes our consciousness and the matter our body as well as the phenomenal world. As such, where is death? Then, why to be remorseful?

Sri Krishna further takes us into deeper waters of this wisdom:

All beings were un-manifested before their birth and shall become invisible after their deaths: only in between they appear to be existent; in such a situation why to lament? (2:28)

This concept has been explained by Zen philosophy: Consciousness is present everywhere across time therefore we must dissolve the rigid boundaries of our ego as well as that of the diminutive personality; as if the central point of the circle were present everywhere and its circumference nowhere.

According to the *Advaita* (Non-duality) philosophy also: the base of our consciousness at depth is one; obviously only one power keeps us in divine awareness; meditation and contemplation take our mind nearer to that source of Eternal Power. Only self-realization is potent of unveiling the Truth of the Reality and the essence of life; this brilliance when showered could wash away our grief.

In this context, it is also worth analyzing that even when the body and the brain cease to pulsate, the *Ātman* (Pure Consciousness, Spirit) does not die. Life after death, or reincarnation, does not necessarily mean reappearance of physical body in some other form; it could as well be a newer dimension or extension which gives a different platform to the existence. With reference to the 'time', the 'eternity' can never be conceived! This Eternity happens beyond time. The human time is the product of human mind; hence it is a bonded concept, not eternity. Our ego is afraid of self-destruction therefore we are terrorized by the death.

The root cause of our *Dukha* lies in our ignorance about the concept of time as a whole. On the nutrient of this nescience our ego germinates, proliferates, and then controls our life.

Tyāga, or dispassion, forbearance, austerity is one of the tested method for making the ego disciplined; it means, renunciation from 'I-ness', 'my-ness'; detachment from cynosure or allurement; freedom from arrogance and snobbery, wise surrender of which, most of the time, remains busy in the search of selfish satiation. If you 'stand' apart from yourself and watch carefully, how your ego keeps on manipulating for fulfillment of its sensuous desires – you may understand the real nature of your ego. The saintly person abandons his vanity, lives actively in the world yet does not possess a desire for reward of action for self. He does action for the sake of duty, not for selfishness. His intentions are neither to meet the desired nor to plan for indulgence. He does only that for which he receives directives from the Higher Force. Service and surrender are the undercurrent goals of his life.

In this way, when the darkness of ignorance dissolves, the ego starts behaving as a benevolent supporter – and the root cause of sufferings come to an end. Thus, one understands that immortality is a quality of existence, not that it is an extension of one's permanence to remain alive in the same body for ever along the arrow of time.

The immortality or *Amaratva* (no death) can never be visualized by means of ordinary measurement of time. 'To always remain alive is not immortality – this will become a curse! To be alive always – immortality – is to be a time transcendence being, to go beyond time, to merge the self (*Jeevātma*) into the Cosmic Self (*Parmātma*), to dissolve our boundaries. When a person achieves this dynamic awareness, he gains freedom from the clutches of time. Thereafter, he neither laments about the past happenings nor gets perturbed by the futurity; he 'lives' in the present – in the 'Now'.

About *Klesha* (sorrows), Sri Krishna says, the men who do not nurture faith and cultivate real knowledge of the truth, always convolute in the middle of angst and dejection.

अज्ञश्चाश्रद्दधानश्च संशयात्मा विनश्यति।
नायं लोकोऽस्ति न परो न सुखं संशयात्मनः।।

(4:40)

The ignorant, the faithless, the skeptics ones are destroyed; there is neither this world, nor the other, nor happiness for the one who doubts.

The person who is entangled in the net of doubts, and who lacks self-confidence, can never be free and fearless. In the midst of petty anxieties, such a person is stung by pain all along his life's journey.

The Gitā further illumines the nature of *klesha*:

One, who performs righteous actions, never faces depressive state of mind – in future also, because it is the present which creates the future.

One, who purifies karma by consistent efforts, hits the highest target.

The person, who completely cleans his mind, never enters in the realm of weary-way.

'Time' is the expression of the Almighty. The time performs the drama of creation and dissolution.

The wheel of birth and death goes on rotating non-stop, whether you wish it or not!

Keeping this truth in the mind, it makes wisdom to go on struggling with patience, to win over the negativity and to live one's life cheerfully as well as happily.

By practicing Sādhnā (devotion) in continuum, with tranquil mind, the Self shines forth in your being.

In case one feels difficulty in practice, then one must act for the highest cause; by doing so the mind remains serene.

Even if performance of one's duty creates uneasiness, one must surrender the fruits of karma by self-control; thus not worrying about the fruition, the toil generates peace into the life of the doer.

Dimensions of pure knowledge are: absence of self-praise even at the time of great achievements, non-violence, clemency, simplicity of mind and speech, faith, cleanliness, equipoise, and discipline of sensuous desires.

Passion, birth, old age, disease, death, etc., are the source of sufferings, twinge and twitch; therefore, one should not get upset by such situations.

Lack of intensive attachment with progeny, life partner, property and wealth generates peace. In the face of finding oneself in conducive or repulsive situation, one has to remain even-minded.

Devotion to the Creator, to live in solitude, and to avoid the company of sensuous person, and regular study of, and contemplation upon, spiritual knowledge shall make you a pristine pure being.

These virtues carry, extended meanings; every point of wisdom should be absorbed with its essence. The target is to decipher the structure of suffering, to identify its original spring, and to protect ourselves from these pains and malaise so as to live a life: complete and abundant.

Check the speed of wind!

For most of us it appears to be an enigma to control the mind, to suppress desires, to monitor tendencies, and to check the onslaught bashing by sensuality, anger, proud, greed, etc.; the power-packed forces. While living in the society, amidst its absurdities, such exercise, i.e. control of mind, does not appear to be practicable. To a certain degree, such thinking could be justified, but the advice of the wise should be taken for their deeper connotations; not merely in their literal sense. An intelligent person with a well-rounded personality does not try to crush his desires or to subdue the mind; he watches them intently and awakened, he analyses their fabrication. A sharp observer tries to perceive character, nature and organization of his own propensity as well as the mind, and diagnoses the cause of his pains which trickle down from them.

Thereafter, the knowledgeable acts in the world, balances his expressions and steers his *karma* towards duty, integrity and rectitude. Such an awakened person does not try to demolish his longings; on the contrary, he dissects them, grasps their motives and thinks about the adverse outcome in case such desires were attended to. Experiencing every fact of life, the alert person never gets sucked up by passion and bindings of the worldly affairs or things. By identifying the origination of suffering, pain and sorrows, he blocks the vexation at its source itself.

It is pivotal to know that if someone identifies his own *'real nature'* then he could dissolve his limiting boundary of existence, and evolve a supportive ego.

A disciple questioned Buddha: "How can we save a drop of water from getting dried up?"

The Tathāgat answered: "By throwing it into the sea!"

Clear as it is: if you want to save your life from being wasted, merge it with the Infinite Cosmic Power!

Thence, no fear, no suffering, no pain, no dejection can overpower you, because you get unified with the *Sat, Chitta, Ānanda* (Truth, Awareness and Pleasure).

Thus, all could be attained by changing oneself with ease. No upheaval, no horse-riding, all spontaneous; if only once the enlightenment showers upon your being. All fears setting down, all happiness arising up!

Knowledge of the 'Knowledge'

First we must understand: what is the knowledge; then only we may know what is ken (pristine wisdom). News bulletins, information or extensive data is not 'ken' or pure, uncorrupt Knowledge. To know about the worldly affairs is only a communication of general information but not realization. The cognizance of Truth is an experience of much higher level. There are two aspects of perception: One, what we know through our sense organs, and the other, what lies behind that thing as reality. To see the unveiled truth of relationship between these two aspects is the real 'seeing', or uncontaminated knowledge, or ken.

Therefore, whatever we have taken for granted and fixed it into our psyche labeling it to be a 'fact', has to be 'cleaned', erased, rubbed off, or washed away. Then only, on the screen of pure, innocent mind, it might become possible to write the script of realization of the Truth. And, then only we could understand our life as well as the world in which we live.

If someone knows a subject or technique in an expert way, he may freely work in that area of activity, but suppose he knows nothing about the job then that person is subjected to constraint of uncertainty. In the same way, if we could put our fingers on the pulse of our sufferings, we may know their cause, and ultimately get rid of them.

The Game of Fate

There is no comprehensive philosophy or logical explanation for fatalism which could convince about the *modus operandi* of destiny. All depends upon our mental state; in such circumstances in which we find ourselves helpless and incapable of doing anything, we call the happening a 'game of the fate'. In a way this reasoning is not wrong because when we feel that we are powerless and ineffective, we naturally tend to seek solace in 'luck'. The concept of fatalism or destiny provides a ground for patience and courage. But when we are fully capable to handle the situation, and select our action freely, we abandon the idea of fate. Then the responsibility of its outcome also lies upon our shoulders. We cannot escape the good or bad results of our deeds. Our *karma* will flower and bear fruits as well.

With the above context, the philosophy of *Karmayoga* (the yoga of action) remains the best approach. So, don't leave anything on fate; let it play its game while you play yours; continue to act and never get excited or worried about the fruition of your action. Surrender fruits of the works at the altar of the Almighty!

Diagnose the root cause of sufferings and then by hard, sincere and right action uproot the weeds. Our ego is very clever; it always confuses our intellect; we even cannot get a glimpse of that ego unless we chase it with intent concentration and mindfulness. We don't know our 'self' still we think that we know ourselves in-and-out. The day we recognize this aspect of our individuality, it will be the day of our enlightenment!

These days, we could learn how brave people dare to come out of calamity. In December 2004, the southern region of Andman–Nicobar Islands was devastated by the Tsunami hurricane; the dance of death lasted for a day and night; several hutments and villages were swallowed by the sea. Thousands of humans and animals were killed or lost in the rage. Families were eradicated. Then, after a few days, torrential rains lashed the whole area for several days. Then the 'anniversary' i.e. 26th December 2005! Memory revisited the place at the end of one year of the holocaust. Then Christmas, New Year as well as a terror of recurrence of Tsunami!

But look at those courageous, calm and enduring warriors who survived from the bloody claws of dreaded death, and now say – "We will not mourn on the anniversary; we will celebrate for those who escaped and are living today. We will dance and feast on Christmas and New Year – to rekindle a new hope. Life is flowing. Sun is shining. New life is taking birth. *Newly-born are smiling!*

The game of the fate
And awareness of action
Depend on faith and optimism;
And announce the end of the sorrows.

•

Symphony - 2

The Pristine Knowledge

According to Lord Buddha, ignorance is the main cause for all the sorrows in the world; but we should not interpret this declaration as: 'if we shed off all our ignorance, we may achieve wisdom'. By rubbing off any negativity from life, the positivity does not originate by itself; it needs perseverance to cultivate, to germinate and to rear carefully all the newly born virtues; then, we have to nourish them throughout the remaining days of our life.

The first step on the ladder to achieve the pure knowledge is to realize our own ignorance. How shallow we are in our awareness? How much darkness prevails in the inner chambers of our being? One who perceives that he knows almost nothing about the life and the Self, he might think of reaching to the door of wisdom. Else, not!

We always live in an erroneous notion that we are *Gnyāni* (knower of the Truth), or we are more enlightened than the rest. But such a delusion about the self is far from the truth. Therefore, if you wish to enter the kingdom of blissful ken, first of all accept that you are least aware about Truth and Reality.

Here, we are not talking about the 'know-how' about street smartness, science, technology, finances, politics, sociology or all and sundry subjects; and neither Buddha meant to express about such mundane knowledge. All these data, information and physical facts are, no doubt, necessary for our existence; the practical skill and scientific systems are essential for our security, material needs, comforts and dynamic ascent of our life.

But, with regard to our *Klesha* (sufferings) or 'dimensions of unhappiness', we are talking about the 'spiritual crisis' or 'catastrophe of consciousness' – and about enlightening or en-darkening related to these eventful sectors of life. We can name such glorious knowledge as '*Cognition of the Truth*' so that it could be conceived in isolation from worldly general knowledge.

Search for the Truth

We must continue to discover that the 'cognition of the Truth' can unveil the phenomenal reality of our existence, and which is capable of introducing us to the God, *Ātman* and Nature, ushering into multidimensional power of these supra-mental brilliances. Also we need to have an extraordinary illumination which can penetrate into intensive darkness and expose the transparent nature of our mind before us. Such a radiating *Gnyān* could make our life tranquil, and connect us with the *Paramātma*, the absolute energy, cosmic intelligence and infinite *Pragyā* (*Viveka*, discriminative intellect).

It is not difficult to experience the cognizance of the Truth; it continuously gets dispersed all around us, in Nature, cosmos, animates and inanimate, atoms and particles, our mind, intellect, ego, the Self; and in the Glow of the Almighty! The insight for such awareness could be connected with the Cosmic Knowledge; in other words, the insight of the Truth is the extension of that *Infinite Ken.* After this revelation, where remains a need to search Him?

Sant Kabir sings: "Only he finds who dares to enter the deep waters". Kabir is neither talking about an imaginary god, nor of any godhead who is posted on a diamond-studded throne. He is pointing out at *Gyāna*, Realization of the Truth, righteous law of life, and uncorrupt, innocent nature of our Self.

The incoming information and sensations through the media of our sense organs accumulate a specific sort of knowledge – this remains only mechanical, physical or digital, if we don't churn it and filter it to take out the essence, and if we don't see the intrinsic value of the element. On viewing mechanically, suppose a desirable beautiful object is seen which instigated our desire to possess that; this is the beginning of agitation but in that high tide we could not watch the beauty, delicacy, charm and grace of that thing or person. We could not touch the inner-core bliss because we were stuck up in the darkness of desire. Whatever we could comprehend it was the outer morphology, shape, size, dimension or geometry of the object – its existential presence. But alas! We could not decipher that element in the object which in reality it 'was'!

Mostly, in such scenario our mind remains engulfed in the dirty layers of our longings. Such visions go on changing every moment and are always encountered in life yet we show to be happy like a blindfolded mortal!

Buddha advises that at the baseline level of our life, contemplation, meditation and practice to develop authority of mind over matter can help to take us from ignorance to the blissful state.

Five-step Contemplation

Reflection on compassion: Think of pain and sufferings of animates; sprout clemency towards them.

We remain, mostly, indifferent towards troubled humans and other living beings; or, at the most we verbally express our concern. If by contemplation on mercy or compassion, we were to awake our feelings of compunction, our conscious awareness extends unrestrictedly, and we feel to offer selfless service to the destitute. This act fills our life with unparallel fulfillment.

Contemplation upon love: Develop intense emotion in your heart so as to wish welfare of all beings of the world.

Pray for your enemies so that they may be blessed with right thinking; in this way they could receive some happiness. Also, living in modern troubled surroundings, beside prayer, some practical contribution to lessen the trouble in the world is urgently required.

Contemplation upon Bliss: Wish for wellbeing of all. Be happy to see the prosperity and pleasure of others.

If someone has progressed by righteous hard-work, be delighted; with such a mind-set, the negative tendencies, like – jealousy, hatred, enmity, agitation, etc., cannot make their nest in your heart. Beside this, a feeling of peace and prosperity for the world also develops in your mind.

Reflection on impurity: Think about the painful outcome of unrighteous actions.

By thinking about negativities in life, one may visualize a horrid picture of the results of malign *karma* which may warn us at the time of our weakness to commit blunder. Such a caution acts effectively.

Contemplation upon tranquility: Practise this aspect of meditation – your mind will rise above the conflicts within.

Pairs of opposite elements *(dwanda)*, such as, poverty-affluence, hate-love, gain-loss, fame-infamy, etc., could be tamed. Thus your mind attains serenity.

The seeker, thus, does not complain about own situation. He continues doing his duty without anxiety.

Four-step Meditation

Solitude: *Ekānta*, a technique to free the mind from clutches of senses.

Equilibrium: *Sthirtā*, control of mental vibration, pours enthusiasm and pleasantness in your ambience.

Spirituality: To feel ecstasy – the Bliss Absolute by way of deep meditation and absorption *(Samādhi)*.

Purity and peacefulness: *(Mahāshānti):* By this meditation, our mind attains its uncorrupt, original nature and becomes ripple-less.

By four types of practice, given below, the power of *Riddhi* (hold of mind over matter) could be achieved. It is practised:

To stop germination of non-virtuous traits,

To uproot those lower tendencies which are firmly implanted in psyche,

To cultivate newer goodness,

To continue search for Truth.

We may redefine these advices and give meanings which suit to the modern times. Live fully in the world; walk on the rock-solid ground of reality with an eye on the absurdity of the present day systems; decorate your thoughts with beautiful pearls of wisdom.

This is the Awareness of pure knowledge.

Analysis of the Abstract Path

In the minds of most of the people, the same questions go on creeping – what is the justification of these sermons or preaching for the man living in complexity of modern times? How can they be useful, effective and practical in supporting our efforts towards survival? How many persons can afford time, or even think about contemplation, meditation, reflection, practice of spirituality while struggling amid the tornado of materialism, marketing, newer parameters for sensuality, natural instinct for keeping oneself alive, infidelity and loss of faith? And if at all someone thinks he does so either in an intensive crisis or during the old age because of fear of the death! This is irrational!

How can those people wish for benediction and happiness of all animate beings that have no time from their own selfish welfare? They remain indulged in satiation of innumerable desires, for unlimited power and influence on others, greed for redundant wealth and a dream of super dominance. And if some people seem to be walking on the path of charity and philanthropy, they mostly desire for name, fame or dignity in society or a dream of heaven. Only a few adapt to a path of non-violence in thought, speech and action. Obviously, the ancient treasures of wisdom are overflowing with the knowledge of the Truth and *Vivek*, yet the inner chambers of modern man are mostly lying empty. As a result they have little happiness and peace.

It can't be imagined, how some persons can react positively, towards prosperity of other people. Can they be pleased in a natural manner? We generally congratulate others on their success but in some corner of our mind there sits a hazy guilt of jealousy. Or, if we show mercy towards someone who is a destitute and helpless weakling, we feel a bit of solace in our painful nodes of life; we intent to fulfill some of our dirty selfishness by such act in which our ego receives a high. We feel unsecured and hence we wish peace and happiness for the whole world. The rest of the tall talks are rhetorical! Most of such things happen against the backdrop of narcissism: the selfish ego!

All are aware about the outcome of bad deeds; even fools know: what happens when we act in a negative way. Maybe, one is not afraid of hell but the natural instinct always subtly points out towards the result of injustice. In spite of this, day-in-and-day-out several persons are engaged in unrighteous activities, yet showing the usefulness of such misdeeds; they put a mask of angelic look on the ugly faces of their nefarious acts.

Under this setup of affairs, the mental conflict generates real tsunami typhoon. It appears to be impossible to escape that horror: two opposite poles of *Dwanda* emerge and torture. They are repulsive to each other, though always existing together!

We know, understand and are aware about the remedy of such conflicts but we rarely dare to walk on the path of duty, morality and justice.

Hence, the question pops up: Have the philosophy of Buddha and, for the same reason, other wisdom of ancients lost their power, effect or relevance?

Before answering this hard question, we must perceive that the pristine flow of ken springs forth when the seeker establishes himself in deep meditation upon the Cosmic Intelligence. In other words, although seemingly the stream of true knowledge gushes from the minds of great saints (*Mahātmā*), in actuality it expresses the celestial source of omniscience, or we can say – it is the manifestation of the Cosmic Intelligence through the medium of the knowledgeable sages.

Since millennia, such blitz of flashes has been enlightening the meditative minds; they usher the humanity in the path of

Reality and Bliss Absolute. It is clear that the question of their being effective, ineffective or righteous is an erroneous enquiry because such teachings are eternal truth. They don't need the help of any other so-called 'truth' for their re-establishment. Yet, of course, for conditioning to fit in the changing times, these gems of wisdom might be fashioned anew.

With this facet in view, we muse:

To help the under-trodden; as far as possible,

No place for hatred and jealousy in our life,

From time to time thinking about the fruits of ill-deeds,

Try to remain balanced in ups-and-downs.

To watch the force and speed of sensual longings and also the agitation created by them,

Always try to remain in pleasant mood,

Enlarge the sphere of spiritual knowledge by studying scripture,

Remain in an innocent, clean and tranquil state of mind,

Continue the search for Truth in life,

Make yourself a calm and presentable personality.

These ten points make an abstract of forgoing discussions out of which even if, to start with, only one trait is followed sincerely, the others will follow slowly to enrich life. Effort is the key.

The teaching of Buddha is timeless as well as timely, not an absurd rhetoric. It is most urgently required today when onslaught and character-disintegration is going on; to save humanity from demoniac magic; and to survive the tsunami cyclones within our being.

Expanse of our Mind

Ordinarily, we believe that our mind knows everything; it can reach every nook and corner, as it is an extremely swift traveler it can enter the past and run towards the future at the same time. It can put up the intricate details of the world within no time: instantaneously! We believe this and we take it for granted: our mind extends into enormously vast magnitude; it can penetrate through time-space to decipher the reality of existence!

But it is not true. Our mind is ignorant about several aspects of our personal world. Obviously, in so far as awareness is concerned, it jumps within ignorance. And our original definition says that ignorance is the root cause of *Dukha* (sufferings). Hence the mind catches on sorrow – even swimming in the redundant material luxury! Once Bob Green mentioned the following: "When you do not know that, in actuality, what you want, then you end up in a situation which you like the least."

What we do not know? In the world, all-through the life we come in contact with innumerable people, but we cannot know their mind, their inner thoughts or feelings. We can never perceive, what goes on in the infinite depth of their heart; of course, this is a different matter that we may get some idea of their thinking by their body language; still we remain in doubt! Therefore, it has to be verily accepted that even in intimate relationship, in the society, or at the work place where mostly we come in close contact with people, we cannot decipher the structure of minds and flow of thoughts in other persons.

In addition to this, we cannot understand the micro-level continuous change in the world: not always and not immediately. Think! What is happening in the outer world at this particular moment? What sort of transformation and alterations are taking place? In which direction Nature is active to produce something anew? Who is where? What are they doing? Many more, innumerable questions! Although, our mind can imagine from here; that it generally does; but can never visualize the reality, unless the events or systems do not happen in our presence. Or, when every happening has happened, then only we experience a bit of its warmth.

After all, the fields of our mind remain circumscribed, and at the end of the event also, the knowledge of things remains subjective – only for our consumption. In spite of this fact, we go on thinking that our mind is super fast, super powerful, vigorous and fiery; it cannot be controlled!

It is super fast, no doubt, but it is restless, agitated, and jittery-like a monkey; in addition, it is ignorant, incapable of living in serenity. Not omniscient.

In the same context, this also appears to be true that no other person can ever know my pains, in totality, since they also take birth in the extension of my mind: personal grief, sufferings, dejections, frustrations, love, hate… and a long list of emotions! My agony and ordeals are specific and unique to me – then, how can they be known by the minds of others?

What am I looking at? No one can see my 'seeing'. What mind is churning? This can never be a subject of understanding for others.

Such is the chaos and disarray of 'knowing' and webbings of mind. In this confused state of affairs, we are challenged to wake up the 'Awareness of profound knowledge'. The ancient sages have shown us the way: *Only by connecting with the Energy of 'Ātman' (the brilliance of the Self) one can attain the state of pure, uncontaminated knowledge about the Supreme.*

Fulfillment by Way of Realization and Ken

After knowing both the facets of mind, we learn that all the *kleshas* originate from the mind; it is quivering, unstable, ignorant about several affairs but, at the same time, we may attain wisdom, peace and freedom only through the mind as an instrument; this exposes the bright side of *chitta* (mind, intellect, ego, self-sense in totality).

We can live our life in the world effectively if we mentally become well-organized and if we could train our mind rightly. This is so because without the help of the mind we cannot get rid of the clutches of mind. And without such freedom we cannot do proper action, or attain devotion, knowledge, even *Nirvāna* – the freedom.

It is also urgent to know clearly that our thoughts could be irrational and unrighteous at times; we become confused, live in uncertainty, commit slippages, or go on weaving wrong notions. Hence, the sages of the world religions have blessed the humanity by showing pathways to keep the mind silent and serene. These methods could be broadly designated as *meditation*: in meditation, we do not trample the mind; neither tame it to be obedient. Rather it is made to enter the realm of dynamic quietude. Even then, the mind shows its power to move very fast, and remains alert. Occasionally, it dissolves itself in the absolute calmness, which is the world of pure 'Nothingness'. Nothing remains thereafter to be achieved anymore. The upheaval of entire pain and pleasure transforms into dynamic silence. Live with mindfulness!

Thus, when the mind attains innocence and uncorrupt state, our Self or *Ātaman*, reflects brightly. In other words, only through immaculate, dirt-free mind, the rays of our *Ātaman* can disperse upon our life – not through the contaminated webs of thoughts. We know our world around us, and also ourselves, only against the backdrop of our experiences which are flowing as uninterrupted stream through our life. One after the other, the impressions of events, continue to paint the canvas of our *chitta*. Our existential void could be fulfilled if we prudentially scan such incoming experiences and then only absorb or store the selected ones within our being. These two main revelation – experience (or realization) and intent observation of existence in its entirety – groom our personality. Within the spheres of *realization of the truth* and un-flickering *awareness*, our conviction, faith, true knowledge, devotion towards the Creator, love, creative potentiality and holistic completeness evolve, come to flowering and fruition, and disperse fragrance all around.

This makes the meaning of life; our purpose of coming on to this planet is fulfilled and our karma is synthesized; freedom and grace of the God are showered. The whole system of cyclic movement rotates on the axle of the mind. Hence, walk on the way of "balance the one – all others will be balanced by themselves". And, therefore, harmonize and synchronize your mind!

Beyond the Time

We normally feel that the time passes on, goes on, or moves on uninterruptedly in a linear fashion; it appears so because incessant alterations perpetually happen in our body, in Nature and consequently in our life, But this we know through our feelings, sensations or reasons. Every creature receives different impression of time duration. All is relative – not absolute!

Clear as it is, only our mind realizes the varied speed of time. In effect, the time neither 'walks' nor remains stationary. The time 'is' – that's all!

The wise sages who unveiled the technique of meditation could know this fact. If our mind comes to a state of total quietude, we can cross the limit of time. We can enter the transcendental regime of the universe. There lies the kingdom of divine; there lies silence; awareness is there but no wave. Only our mind can take us beyond time, where freedom, or *Moksha*, or *Nirvāna*, reigns supreme.

Only by way of our realized knowledge, we may be able to imbibe the manifested 'Truth' and 'Existence' within; we can as well make our intuition sharper and credible, and extend the horizon of our intellect. The invaluable treasure of our experiences helps us to scan our objectivity – that means, the continual flow of wisdom can unveil the reality about events, things or persons; otherwise we go on evaluating the world on the basis of our 'firm' beliefs and convictions – and mostly we are mistaken. Even then, we take our wrong identification as a truth! Such knowing exists in the field of 'subjectivity': confined, delimited. Our own idea; not the reality of the things!

We do not create the whole world but still we go on creating our own limited world on the basis of our conditioned reasoning and biased experiences. Therefore, catch hold of logic, justice and righteousness. This is the secret of attaining success and getting peace and fulfillment, and the technique to get rid of sufferings!

•

Resonance – 2

My mental threads and fibers fine –
Weave my world, possessed by none,
Pain and pleasure and dreams are mine,
How do I tell my secret to someone?

The light can enter not within –
Till it is solid dark and dim,
But at the moment of flash of blitz,
The Truth does come to prevail within

In love, in silence, in blissful calm –
Ponder upon the peace, to meditate,
Don't dance on desires' tune,
Look up high at divine state,

Root of suffering lies; where?
In this chameleon quivering life,
Nothing is immortal, stable, lasting
In the dancing flickering vibe!

My world is real, a solid truth,
Embedded in the Cosmic Illusion,
It is not eternal, not for ever,
As dancing waves; in fast motion.

Ego adds sorrow for itself,
Make the mind a sharing friend,
With truth, mercy and deeper faith,
Wander in bliss from beginning to end.

Body is the matter, life is energy,
Body dissolves but life flies high
At every point of cyclic time –
Lies ecstasy: enjoy on earth, in the sky!

•

Take in a Stride – 2

Dump the unfriendly one, or remain indifferent towards such persons.

Find the truth by penetrating intellect.

Be alert in all spheres of life.

Who am I not? What is not my nature?

Contemplate on the query.

You are an assembly of energy, hence you are indestructible.

Don't try to trample the mind.

Live lightly, not with heavy heart.

Jubilate, celebrate and laugh!

Dissolve the limiting boundaries of your personality.

Practice of moral courage makes our ego disciplined.

Get out from the dark lanes of arrogance about your high religion, social status, knowledge or wealth.

Structure of Karma

All-through the life, most of humans face extremely complicated and difficult twists and turns and curves, and feeling of emptiness; somewhere in their heart they get sensation as if several dimensions of their existence have remained unfilled: even though they have amassed and are custodians of ample wealth. Regarding such sense of want, or scarceness, every person thinks differently, but even then in one or the other corner of their mind, some sort of void exists and, at times, that pinches acutely.

Fulfillment is a mental state, not an objective phenomenon. It is clear with the fact that the mind within, and the world without: both the spheres go on changing every moment. Both are impermanent as well as transient in nature. Then, how to solve the equation of completeness? How could we experience a crowning validity of our existence or purpose of our being alive?

We can do it by –

Performing actions in probity,

Not worrying about the future,

Adjusting the self in conformity with the changing arrangements of life-factors,

Becoming polite and humble,

Being optimistic,

Having clear vision of the goal of life,

Keeping patience and courage at the time of crisis,

Understanding desires, and by

Connecting the Self with the Almighty.

Generally we know about the essence of these nine points but we do not see the glimmering indication that action (*Karma*) is the most powerful element of our purpose in life. All paths are connected with *Karma* – the creative energy, and in the end it is the *Karma* which unites us with the God.

Based on a true incident the following shows *Karmā*:

Pāthakji is a farmer with a small holding; he works very hard for livelihood to sustain his family. He loves to listen about spirituality and Gitā. Whenever there is a discourse on these subjects, he attends the event.

One day, a learned person came to the village. He was talking about, how Arjuna kept his bow-and-arrows down, and never wanted to fight the war of Mahābhārata; how Sri Krishna explained about the 'right of action but not in its fruits'. Pāthakji was listening intently. The dialogue ended in the late evening – at about 11.

And, at about 1 O'clock, it started raining very heavily, followed by hailstorm. The village farmers were caught in the grip of anxiety, as the crop was almost ready for harvesting.

In the early morning Pāthakji went to his farm, with pounding heart. Lo! Most of the crop was destroyed. He sat in the field, with head down in dejection, hopelessly. For about an hour his mind was blank! But suddenly he remembered Arjuna's bow, the Gāndeev, and the 'fruition of karma' as narrated by Sri Krishna!

He got up. Calm! Alert! And he started his work to face the calamity.

This is the real Brilliance of Knowledge!

According to Buddhism, every person is a Buddha, or enlightened one, right from his birth; hence he must work in life as if living in a post-enlightened state. And he must express gratitude towards the Creator that he was already a *Gyāni* at the time of his birth: innately! By keeping this wisdom in our bosom we may keep the degrading acts away.

The fundamental teaching of Zen reveals – *'To act on the solid ground of reality is superior to imaginary thoughts'*. In other words, one must be practical, absorbed in whatever worldly job one is doing, without thinking about philosophical implications or metaphysical matter at that time. This is the attainment of Zen.

It could as well be interpreted: we must understand the utilitarian and applicable aspect of the theoretical knowledge; the hypothetical or suppositional learning must be deeply searched for some essence in them which could practically enhance the quality of human life. If one is successful in such an effort, one is said *to be in the Zen*.

The teaching of Zen parallels with that of the *Gitā*. If we do not float above the ninth cloud, and continue to work hard to face the real problems in life, we can attain freedom. We can never control our future; even we don't know anything about it!

Further, it has been declared about *karma*, the dynamics of action: Intuition, innate prudence, or uncorrupt, unconditioned intellect is better than the learning through information or iron-jacketed education, without practical experience. Develop a specialized skill to *analyze* an event instantaneously, without muddling with illogical cobweb!

Intuition is 'superior' to the 'said' or 'heard' knowledge. The action performed on the basis of 'inner voice' generally remains within the circumference of justice and freedom. If our intellect remains uncontaminated by sludge of the world, our intuition can never act negatively.

Basic innocence of the self takes birth from the womb of serene *chitta*, not from the agitated one. It is revealing that our thoughts are structurally immaculate as well as free from dirt, but since they pass through the thick of our desires, they suddenly get tarnished.

If we could understand this fact, then our *karma* (actions) will always be *sukarma* (benevolent acts).

Architecture of our Experiences and Karma

While acting in the world outside, we are heavily armed with our experience. We work or react only by the instigation of our acquaintance and familiarity with the subject through our experiences, irrespective of the fact whether they are from the past, or of the present, or spill out from the subconscious or unconscious mind. The whole drama is played against the backdrop of desires and ego.

We cannot have cognizance of happenings and things of the world without prompting of our prior setup of mind about that situation. Our sense organs are powerful enough to absorb the incoming sensations, but they are incapable of influencing our experiences and thought-flow. It is our mind alone, which acts towards stimuli and then decides to do *karma*.

The kaleidoscopic collage of the world goes on altering in a fast-forward mode; and incidences of all kinds are perpetually happening, but what is that power which acts behind them, we do not know! Under such volatile situations, we continue to decide for undertaking actions. And if we do not act with a sharp acumen of awareness, we land in confusion. We commit disgraceful slippages in our *karma.*

Therefore, we must always arrange and rearrange our experiences in a meticulous manner. We must classify them and then only select the suitable; otherwise, our life will be lost in the rampant crowd of the inflow of impressions and emotions. Sri Aurobindo showed a way to freedom:

"All life is the play of universal forces. The individual gives a personal form to these universal forces. But he can choose whether he shall respond or not to the action of a particular force. Only most people do not really choose – they indulge in the play of forces. Your illness, depression, etc., are the repeated play of such forces. It is only when one can make oneself free of them that one can be the true person and have a true life – but one can be free only by living in the divine."

We may also think that too much of practical approach in life may give rise to a mechanized thought-flow: Purely technical! We make a target, then, we toil to achieve that. But only by such karma, our conscience cannot evolve in its multi-format because the target was purpose-built and also tailored by our desires.

The courtship between mind and *karma* is strange:

If you are bewitched by something or someone, or, you are smitten by single track obsession for any work, it may happen that at some point of time you start trying to get rid of that. This is an instinct of survival or escaping.

While hooked-up with societal customs, or abiding by practicality of life, we ignore looking at values of humanity.

Assess your position objectively and examine it with a view-point of evaluation, then do action.

Preaching on morality and decisions based on mental ideation must be applicable in practice; if they are not useful, think that the teachings are weak in some way.

Those karmas are meritorious which give maximum of happiness and peace to maximum number people.

Virtuous karmas are graceful and universally the same but dirt of our mind distorts their elegance. Our actions must have some day-to-day utility as well.

Our mind (*Chitta*) is always busy in the search of newer fields of activities for its own pleasure. It creates such a glimmering magic which we take to be the goal of our life. Under the hypnotic influence of that magic we go on revolving in the frenzy of redundant activity in this world; and thus end up as an accumulator of all sorts of *karma*. At the same time, we forget that the energy of each *karma*, gets condensed and then attached to our consciousness.

Whichever thing we consider to be useful for our selfish gratification, we make it our object of fulfillment; that takes the form of the ultimate purpose of our life, the meaning of our existence! But we do not perceive that if we chase the pleasure for self-seeking ends, it dodges us; it can never be taken hold of.

If we go on turning and twisting in the drain of our self-indulgence, we can never accumulate virtuous and sanctified *karmā*. Beside this, a person who is very 'clever' and bursting with pride, remains unable to think about the knowledge of the Self, or *Ātmagyān*, because he has his own long term planning to fulfill the wild desires; and so he fails to divert his mind away from personal motives and private ends. It is a great surprise that such a person, engrossed in self-love, even after attaining his goal goes on sweating and gasping with open mouth on the same degrading track. Blind-folded pony with massive load of desires on his back!

Therefore, to clean the scum, an unpleasant substance that forms on the surface, in life. The wise have kindly given direction that we must escort our ego out of the narrow, dark lanes of narcissism and meander it towards highways of goodness to all. There exists a deep relationship between virtue and happiness. The real ecstasy could be achieved only by functional service to all beings and to Nature. This, in its own right, connects people through invisible but strong strings of love and kindness which, in the end, generate bliss and beatitude in our being.

A person who is mentally infested with negativity is seldom cordial and friendly to others; he becomes emotional and prideful, lacks sensitivity and mercy. The negative thinker acquires arrogance, and remains adamant on his evil acts. Then, how can he think about virtuous *karma*?

It is clear, that a false conviction about our own behaviour and action, even if they are detrimental, is the mother of all sorrows and sufferings. Such firm beliefs delude us; they are not the reality of affairs. Living in the illusion of our own making, we indulge in visualizing that if we acquire more material luxuriance, we may become happier. In such a circle we revolve all-through the life, but mostly it ends-up in futility. In effect, we love certain things but at the same, we nurture hatred or jealousy against several other 'things' – yet all is served to us as an admixture of 'likings' and 'dis-likings'. Therefore we are not happy!

Keeping these facts in view, we have to take the full charge, or responsibility, of our life to steer it out of the muddle; by keeping our mind, intellect and ego under amicable, subtle control, or discipline, and have to enhance the evolution of life towards a synchronized harmony.

How can we know the essentials of these teachings, the kernel of the wisdom? Most of us know what they convey, but how to imbibe and follow the truth of the wise sayings?

It indicates the state of ignorance, of darkness! If we could develop a cognizance of our shortcomings and the inner vacuum, we may be able to find the direction which leads to real knowledge; the darkness could be dispelled. We have to search, one by one, our inadequacies and failures. This is the first step forward towards a long journey. One tiny change, a small deviation for betterment, acquires an incredible greatness of the desired objective after a passage of time; this phenomenon is a matter of general experience. It also means if we cultivate an intent awareness about our life, we may become capable of seeing through an extensive, multidimensional panorama of our existence.

In accordance with the findings of modern psychology, if a person performs ignoble karma, he develops mental tension, consequently disturbing chemical chain of reactions in his body, and generally becomes a prey of depression which maybe in dormant stage but it erupts as a lava-flow at the time of weaker moment in life.

We have to taste the fruits of our *karma* – whether today or at another stratum of the time. Suppose we don't agree with this proposition, then what? Imagine, if we have not yet received the rewards of our good *karma* in this life –and we die, then what will be the fate of those noble *karma* of ours? Have they been wasted? Likewise, it could be said about the bad *karma* also. Is there no punishment for ill-deeds? Then where is the justice?

Mind and Karma

The structure of mind as well as karma is complex:

We can never know the exact thoughts of another person; we can't have an insight about what is happening in the world – unless the event occurs or 'thing' comes to our notice. Only our experience can uphold us. Our thoughts are not rational all the time; we commit slippages; we get confused or become unsteady.

Wealth and prosperity are not able to influence our state of joy and bliss to a very great extent – not at all beyond a certain standard of material achievement. A study in USA revealed that during the last fifty years, the real income of people has increased by 16 per cent, but the number of very happy persons has declined by 4 per cent.

Materialism is anti-productive: those who keep accumulation of wealth on the top of their priority list, they are much less satisfied and remain unfulfilled in several other aspects of life; this is a mystery!

It is only the inner tranquility which gives maximum happiness; noble *karmas* are supportive in this life, no doubt; beside this, they get deposited as a treasure for future. If you don't believe in incarnation, i.e. rebirth, then take it as a new dimension, or another level of time-space for manifestation of energy of your existence.

Our *karmas* radiate mental energy, the consequence of which force manifests at a right place, suitable time, and appropriate circumstance. Virtuous *karmas* are never sterile; today they may however appear worthless. Modern psychologists also talk about enhancing individuality by way of good *karma*.

Karma in the Gitā

The Gitā is the melodious song of *karma*; it is the source spring of wisdom, art of living, and science of remaining pure and immaculate.

In the following pages, we shall pick up gracious pearls regarding *Karma* from the Gitā:

Karmayoga (The Yoga of Action)

In general term, 'Yoga' means to 'unite', 'get connected'; to be one with some phenomenon or element. *Karmayoga* covers an extensive realm of human activity: The knowledge about the framework of *karma*, causal factors of its origin, nature of the fruits of *karma*, accumulated as well as productive *karma*, the *akarma*, non-action, roasting of the seeds of *karma*, etc.

We shall briefly discuss the most famous verse (*Shloka*) in the Gitā about *karma*:

कर्मण्येवाधिकारस्ते मा फलेषु कदाचन।
मा कर्मफलहेतुर्भूर्मा ते संगोऽस्त्वकर्मणि।।

(2:47)

Your right is to work only, but never to its fruit; let the fruit-of-action be not your motive, nor let your attachment be to inaction.

Humans have a full freedom to perform varied actions of their desire but no one should abandon the action because of fear, lethargy or pride. It is also a fact that no one, as such, can give up actions in this world because his innate nature will not permit him to do so.

We can never have any idea about the rewards of our karma because it is beyond our power to recognize the future and to conceive about the kind, time, place, quality or quantity of our action's fruits; therefore it is an act of stupidity to be agitated, depressed or over-anxious about the consequences of our toil. Therefore –

Act,

Remain non-attached to the rewards of action,

Surrender your work at the altar of the highest power,

Remain balanced in success as well as failure,

Equanimity of mind is known as Yoga,

To discipline the mind by using intellect is known as Yoga of Gyān,

Humans sink into the sticky marshland if they are restless and excited to get beneficial result,

Seeds of karma are roasted if one attains peace of mind; that is, then such seeds cannot germinate,

To act skillfully is yoga.

कर्मजं बुद्धियुक्ता हि फलं त्यक्त्वा मनीषिणः।
जन्मबन्धविनिर्मुक्ताः पदं गच्छन्त्यनामयम्।।

(2:51)

The wise, possessed of knowledge, having abandoned the fruits of their actions, freed from the chain of birth, go to a state which is beyond all evils.

One, who knows the art of living, keeps his mind in a balanced state and abandons anxiety about the remuneration for his exertion and deeds. By this method his ego and the desires instigated by the ego, both become subdued. Once someone gets established in the *Karmayoga,* his ego does not raise its head again to revolt.

Unveiling the deeper meaning of *karma*, Sri Krishna further expounds: No one can ever receive blessings by non-action (i.e. *Sanyās* from work), nor gets any divine power by leaving all actions. Not to perform any action is negativity and it is impossible as well to do so.

Hence, the Gitā advises that men must go on doing their duties with labour; they should keep their attitude justified and evolve the self-being.

The one who forcibly checks one's sense organs and does not perform duties – thinking that this practice is *a yoga of non-action*, yet the mind of the same person continuously visualizes sensuality, he is a hypocrite – a fraud.

On the contrary, one who monitors one's sense to transact with noble deeds and is engaged in *karmayoga*, such a person becomes the custodian of excellence.

Sri Krishna elaborates the significance of *karma*; and thus motivates Arjuna to perform his duties as a warrior:

नियतं कुरु कर्म त्वं कर्म ज्यायो ह्यकर्मणः।
शरीरयात्रापि च ते न प्रसिद्ध्येदकर्मणः।।

(3:8)

You perform your allotted duty; because action is superior to inaction. Even the maintenance of the body would not be possible for you by inaction.

If one does not work laboriously with heart and mind in it, and one who does not exert in doing duties, one may invite trouble for health as well as existence.

The *karma* of service to others and the act with a sense of submission and resignation – i.e., in a non-attached flow, do not put a man in bondage. The Creator of the Universe has desired to create with a feeling of blessing so as to make all the elements of subsistence exist in happiness and peace.

Sri Krishna reassures Arjuna that the practitioner of *karmayoga* achieves the highest target of blissful divine state.

तस्मादसक्तः सततं कार्यं कर्म समाचर।
असक्तो ह्याचरन्कर्म परमाप्नोति पूरुषः।।

(3:19)

Therefore, always perform actions in the spirit of duty – without attachment; for by performing action without attachment, man attains the Supreme.

Do your duties incessantly, perform such actions which are necessary, which is expected from you for benediction of the family as well as the society. But in order to protect yourself from sufferings, you must keep away from passion and attachment towards such actions because *Moha*, or passion, generates wild desires, and desires give birth to pain and agony.

One who perceives the weaving of mind and *karma*, escapes from the upheaval within.

सक्तः कर्मण्यविद्वांसो यथा कुर्वन्ति भारत।
कुर्याद्विद्वांस्तथासक्तश्चिकीर्षुर्लोकसंग्रहम्।।

(3:25)

As the ignorant men act from the attachment to action, O Bharta! So should the wise men act without attachment, wishing the welfare of the world.

The high achiever and the learned one should also attend to even ordinary tasks; they must exert with enthusiasm, persistence and skill. Such acts encourage the younger generation and to put before them an ideal for performing noble rectitude.

Fulfillment by Way of Karma

काङ्क्षन्तः कर्मणां सिद्धिं यजन्त इह देवताः।
क्षिप्रं हि मानुषे लोके सिद्धिर्भवति कर्मजा।।

(4:12)

They, who long for satisfaction from action in this world, make sacrifices to the gods; because satisfaction is quickly obtained from actions in the world of objects.

If a person works towards achieving sensual redundancy, then he acquires all which he desires in a relatively shorter time; therefore, most of the people select this short-cut of lifestyle with degraded approach and ever remain engulfed in the malign tendency of thoughts and actions. But if we are determined, we can accomplish the aim of reaching to a higher status. This can be done by steering the energy of the Self on to the path of realization and grace of the Almighty.

The bondages of *karma* are the causal forces which produce agony and anguish. Sri Krishna prescribes a remedy for this:

Surrender all the actions at the holy feet of the Supreme and demolish all incertitude about the Self and Cosmic Self by using viveka (discriminative sharp intellect).

Such humans can never be enslaved by *karma*; they remain untouched by depression, and their *karma* don't get accumulated, hence can't do harm even, in the future.

Prakriti and Purush

When the elemental Self (*Purush,* Consciousness) comes in contact with Nature *(Prakriti)*, the latter becomes active. Senses, mind and intellect, when combined, give rise to ego. There exists a higher nature above *the nature at lower level*; the higher one is called life energy because of which awareness pervades the world. These two aspects of Nature make the source origin for all; therefore the Absolute is the causal force for birth and death of all. Wrong-doers, scoundrels and confused persons never talk about the goal towards the highest realm; their intellect gets corrupted hence they work according to demoniac tendencies.

Karma: Bhakti and Gyāna Yoga

The deed performed at the body level, which makes our mind to walk on the path of higher of goal – is known as *Karmayoga.* An attempt to make the sentiments and emotions to walk on the path of disciplined contemplation about the Creator is called the Yoga of devotion; *Bhaktiyoga.* All sorts of studies, reflections, meditations and dispassion when practised at the level of intellect, and by means of which our mind may enter the serenity of awareness, is termed as Yoga of knowledge *Gyānyoga.*

Even if one does not act because of illusion of attachment, the innate tendency will forcibly instigate him to do *karma.*

स्वभावजेन कौन्तेय निबद्धः स्वेन कर्मणा।
कर्तुं नेच्छसि यन्मोहात्करिष्यस्यवशोऽपि तत्।।

(18:60)

O Son of Kunti! Bound by your own karma born of your own nature that which, through delusion you wish not to do, even that you shall do, helplessly.

Our won nature and inherent disposition motivate us to work in a particular field. If our mind does not remain in our control, we become the slave of situation and then we may decide not to work at all. But the person, who holds his authority over his mind, remains stable and steady in all situations. Such a person receives enlightenment. The God blesses all creatures with energy to perform *karma* – and also cognitive faculty.

The tsunami typhoons in our mind – sufferings and convulsions – are related to our *karma.* As you sow, so you shall reap! According to the *Gitā*, the main factors of such melodrama are: anxiety about the fruition of action, agitation, doubt about success, and worries. Act! Don't react! Action and reaction make a conflicting pair which never stops its dance.

In modern times, the graphics, which are drawn by 'success gurus', are generally not based on evidences and deeper anlyses. They thrust dry definitions upon us. Their meaning could be harmful to persons who adopt them in their lives. 'Perform actions but do not hope for their fruits' is one example of an interpretation which usually dampens our motivation and enthusiasm for doing action. Many become inactive and get sucked-up in the hell of pittance and depletion. '*Your rights are only in karma but not in its fruits*' –actuality means: you are free to act, but it is futile to worry about its result. The result, or reward, will take birth from the womb of future – and no one can ever perceive the future.

If you are agitated without rhyme and reason, your life energy to perform *karma* will be exhausted. Then, where and how will you succeed? Organize your thoughts; do not allow them to run helter-skelter. Well arranged and systematically classified thoughts are more effective than the haphazard ones. Read, listen and understand all educative matter, then make a bearing-point, a nucleus, of your own from where your *karma* get directives so that your own compass may always show you the direction of your goal – lest you get lost in the way. One North Pole! It is most urgent. The Mental Tsunamis strike one-after-the-other. Survive their bashing by means of the knowledge of the Truth. Bow down at the door of Cosmic Power. This is *Nirvāna*.

•

Symphony – 3

The ferocity of raging tsunamis within and the minting of *karma* without should be synchronized; for this goal, we must understand at the onset that the mental turmoil is closely connected with our past experiences and thoughts. The mind ushers us into actions, and our actions earn happiness or pain for us – while living in this world or even after this life, if you believe! It is interesting to note that every human being believes in the future birth, in one form or another; he may do so by believing in another dimension of time-space, in infinite energy and matter, in the extension of one's personal god, or in any other philosophy. Even having all this wisdom, there pops up a doubt even in the mind of a staunch believer – 'we don't know whether there will be a new life or new existence after the present life; sometimes we hear or read some story but it has hardly any solid proof. Is there all void and nothingness, an infinite darkness after the death?' And so on. In spite of such disbelief and incredibility, we go on believing in incarnation because the fear of death prevails – always and everywhere – in our being; or we go on living in the hope of immortality. If our mind takes shelter under the 'rebirth theory', our desire of living for ever seems to be somewhat fulfilled. And we live happily in the golden castle of our own making. Is it not a good idea?

There is all nothingness, but even then why to deprive ourselves of imaginary pleasure, or vicarious excitement, of remaining alive for a long...long duration of time? Also, a question arises – 'If I leave this world before receiving the sweet fruits of my good acts which I am doing now, or without my knowledge of 'how' and 'wherefrom' I suddenly receive pleasure or pain – what is it all about? Or, right from the birth one happens to be blind, lame, handicapped in some form, mentally retarded, leper, or deaf and dumb – a curse of Nature; and most of the other people are born normal – why so? And many more such questions! Great failure in life, trauma, broken relationship, infamy, loss of immense magnitude, catastrophe; or otherwise – fabulous wealth, redundant luxury, grand success; why someone receives these banes or boons, sometimes suddenly?

If you are interested in knowing the answers of the questions raised above, then you have to have a firm belief in *karma* and rebirth – else, forget such queries!

Power of Karma

If we regularly extend the circumferences of our knowledge and ken, our sufferings become depleted, and a celestial pleasure dawns at the horizon of our life. Beside this, we must drive our *karma* effectively because without doing adequate, result-oriented work and adopting a fertile technology, success may elude us.

Therefore, we must perform such actions which in the very life unfold our full potential and manifest *Purusārtha* –i.e., the strength to earn prosperity, to adapt righteous living, enjoyment in natural ways, and ultimately to earn freedom from all. Such action could make our journey – beyond this birth – a divinely music and a smooth flying in the vast blue sky! For this attainment, we shall look into some blessings so gracefully showered by ancients upon mankind.

Yoga Explained

To work skillfully – is Yoga. In the modern reference: it is a suitable extension and promulgation of your contribution; sharp observation and intellectual awareness; keeping the body fit so that *karma* could be performed; alertness towards anti-social elements, other pit-falls, and trap-doors; balanced relationship and contacts in the society; emotional equilibrium, steadfastness, acumen, and impetus to start newer undertakings; yet without egotistic air; concentration, zeal and vivacity to work; firm belief in the Cosmic Power; and laying down of all karma at the feet of the Almighty. In the end of the show, Yoga is to develop non-attachment towards all in order to achieve Freedom, *Moksha*.

Renunciation of the Fruits of Karma

We may say if everyone abandons the desires for the fruits of his action, the functioning of the world may come to a grinding halt. Then in such a situation, how will the entire system of worldly affairs move on? No one would exert if there remains no charm of the alluring reward of one's toil.

Will then, these wisdom directives debase the meaning of all which is said in the scriptures of the world?

To have a clear cognizance of this tangle, one has to contemplate in depth because the structure of *karma* is intricate – made up of inter-connected parts of varied types. One can't perceive it in an ordinary manner. In the foregoing pages we have experienced some glimpses of *karma* in the *Gitā Gyān.*

Now we would talk about its practical aspects:

The brain manifests as mind; the mind produces thoughts which are expressed by speech. The thoughts (*Vichār*) and the speech (*Vācha*) create motivation to perform *karma*. So, *karma* start 'happening', or sometimes even without our understanding of their design, they happen suddenly. If such *karma* produce some unpleasant reactions – such as violence, corruption, sensual indulgence, anger, hatred, shame, depression or any other negativity, then take it for granted that they are *Vikarma* (Demoniac karma). Such *karmas* generate negative energy which drags you into the sludge of agitation, and also produces the wave currents of tsunami in your whole being, which can result into a tornado!

If one deliberately acts to harm others, such *karma* could be troublesome for the doer in this or future lives as well, because particles of guilty conscious and self-condemning feeling get deposited in one's *Chitta;* they tarnish the ego of which dirt the ill-doer can never get rid! The layers of guiltiness are deposited on the unconscious mind of the person who commits misdeed.

Clear as it is, if you do not nourish a strong desire for the fruits of your *karma*, you generally may not indulge in arrant and venomous activity; and if you support the idea of surrendering your fruition of *karma*, will you offer malevolent, discredited, inglorious deeds to the Supreme? Perhaps you may not do so. 'Dispassion in the fruits of *karma*' will then usher into the real meaning – "nothing is mine, I offer unto you what you gave me; I am not losing anything". If this remains the aim of your *karma*, you will never be able to perform shameful actions.

Emotional Waves of Karma

Earlier it was thought that the emotional force weakens our reasoning power. It means, if you act under the influence of highly charged emotions, your intellect slips into background. The reasons become impotent and right decisions could never be taken. But in the recent years, this theory has been rejected and an opposite view is being accepted: "Our emotions and intuitions generally guide our reasoning and usher into the right path, but they do not encourage one to act by themselves."

In spite of this new theory, this remains a fact that emotions, instincts, intuitions and forceful desires could be supportive only when they germinate in the benevolent state of the mental disposition; otherwise they may pull you down, in a ditch. In addition, if you wish to be a virtuous person, you have to cultivate virtues in yourself. On meticulous analysis you may find that each and every aspect in the field of human activities is connected with all other aspects; no unit of karma is independent in itself – for example, if you are not an honest person, you cannot remain untouched by hatred, jealousy, greed, inclemency, anger, manipulation, violence or imbalance. The biggest master-wheel moves all the smaller wheels of a machine.

All rules and all logic we know are made by men or the society, based on partial understanding of the problems of life and the universe. But God's logic or His reasons are not our logic and reasons.

Life is created by the God and rules are created by our logic, that too upon our minuscule knowledge; so they cannot match. The life is natural, the laws are societal, mental.

Nothing is right or wrong, good or bad in the world – that is, such attributes are not given to us by the Almighty. Our mind has stuck such labels on things or happenings. God has given us love and intellect to think ourselves.

Thus, *analyze* the societal laws and don't follow the logic blindly. Understand the rules, see the logic of the Lord and earn compassion and bliss!

Our uncontaminated feelings motivate us to meditate upon the Almighty. Hence, those who do not walk on the right path, do not act judiciously and whose mind are not pure and innocent, for them it becomes difficult to lead a life with kind-hearted disposition. Maybe, they are master-mind in manipulation, and could accumulate fabulous wealth, yet it remains impossibility for them to come out of the void of ultimate non-fulfillment in life.

Consummation of life

We merely visualize the results of our *karma*, next birth, hell or heaven, and causes of our pleasure and pain; or, we define these concepts in chiseled language. Beyond this also, on the basis of our hazy experiences, we propound theories and decorate these theories with religious robes so as to make them more 'unshakable'. But there always remains a lace of doubt in the mind of a person who thinks in terms of scientific analysis: An unending disbelief, a nagging skepticism about the truthfulness of such theories!

However, in spite of living amid such possibilities or uncertainties, we have to search the purpose of our life, or the meaning of this world. What is the final cause, or intent, of our having taken this birth?

Is it merely to eat, drink, sleep, struggle, remain involved in sensuality, and one day to exit? No!

Is it to earn fabulous wealth, fame, power and luxury which may not even lead to a sense of fulfillment in the last phase of life? No!

Is it to remain over busy in such karmas which give birth to self-guilt, a feeling of being a culprit, or insatiable desires? No!

Is it to think high of ourselves in spite of the knowledge that we are mortals, tiny creatures and non entities? No!

Then what?

Think! In the cosmos of infinite dimension, there exist billions and billions of galaxies, out of which in one such vast cluster of celestial bodies, there is one solar system. In this large family of the sun, there is an earth. On this earth you are throbbing as tiny creature which has a life span; not more than the flicker of an eyelid! How much nanosecond? How minuscule in time-space is your micro-existential presence on the planet earth? You are almost a negligible dot of energy, power and capability! May be one billionth!

It is, thus, evident that grandeur in life could be achieved only if we connect ourselves with the Supreme, Omnipotent, Inimitable Grandeur centre of the power; if we merge with that, He and 'I' become one, if we attach ourselves with divine, the truth, infinite Beatitude, Infinite Time then the meaning purpose, aim or reason of life will also become grand and graceful. Such support could only be that of the Cosmic Lord – the Almighty God.

There is only one way to get hooked-up with the root cause of the universe – it is *karma*! Such *karma* which do not chase us to terrorize and do not make us tremble. Only then the purpose of being born can be enlarged like the all pervading sky, transparent and wave-less, else not.

Our day-to-day life is so empty which we try to fill by all sorts of activities, but still our life remains as empty as ever. You take away position, power or money from the individuality of a person; then what is he? He has all to show outwardly but inside he is vacant! Only rare persons have both inner and outer riches!

As such, the fulfillment is impermanent; it vapourizes soon. Yet if we could understand the structure of desires, then the whole problem of fulfillment ceases.

Life is yours, so is the decision, also yours! Hence, to select the positive life-style appears to be justifiable. Foul karma are not created by right actions in the field of knowledge, education, caring for family, literature, music, spirituality, social service, religion, human welfare, environment and, by and large, having interest in supporting the downtrodden. Think! Create your way yourself. Keep high objectives! With all your power and potency, go on expanding the circles of truth, and of happiness to all: in this manner you may find the meaning of your life. Otherwise, it will be an exercise in futility to search the purpose of your existence in the unimaginable vastness of Nature which is functioning in infinite dimensions of energy, time and space; and your life is a negligible flicker of a flash! Dalai Lama asserts: "*First of all, we have to try to improve ourselves in a simple way. Then, side by side, we must help others as far as possible. Also, we ought to accept the possibility that in both types of actions, unpredictable difficulties may arise*."

Chiseled Personality, Skilful Action and Structure of Karma

Most of the time we waste our energy in search of happiness which possesses no form or texture, and we dig in for real pleasure at such places where it is either non-existent or very rare and unstable. We must conceive, in no doubtful term, that even if one is bestowed by fabulous fortune and oozing riches, the wheel of time generally revolves downward, and sufferings may enter the life. The graph of happiness may not always rise upward; it may curb down any time and touch the lowest level. This is a natural tendency, and a law of happiness and unhappiness. Therefore, *one must strike a balance in every situation.* During high tide of good times we should not become arrogant, prideful, self-praising and egotistic; and, during low tide we should not leave the supportive hand of patience, courage, tolerance and good sense. When catastrophe strikes hard, we may lament, cry or become grief-stricken, but as early as possible we have to get out of the mire of sorrow, and try to recondition ourselves to adapt to a new setup of situations.

During harsh times, contemplate upon fate, destiny, divine power, spiritual teachings, philosophical outlook, or laws of Nature. These media of wise thinking will lessen the pain of sting, and calm down the deep agony. This is the method to cultivate skill in worldly affairs as well as to polish individuality.

We go on doing ordinary, absurd activities. But it is better to pay our attention to enhance our personality, groom it from high to higher levels of goodness. We normally take up certain things or acts in an obstinate manner: such as: over-busy in hard labour to assemble more and more material wealth and luxury. But again, a power-packed desire may arise – then again to toil and get agitated to satiate this new monster: an infinite chain of desires and longings!

On this path we earn wrong or right *karma* which, in their turn, again multiply other karma. We remain self-assured if we heap up a conglomerate of worldly luxury, we could get eternal happiness in successive incremental manner; but such thing happens not! If you don't believe this observation, go and investigate the lives of such persons who possess inordinate and exorbitant wealth; and ask them, if they were extremely happy in all nook-and-corners of their life. It is strange that from a distance they appear to be so, but, in reality, it is not so! Of course, it could be possible that they are somewhat better placed than those who are in much lower income-range but it is not possible to grade them 'happy' in the absolute term. The pulse of happiness is not knowable to any one!

Swami Rama adds: "It is better to act according to the directives of intuition, rather than to involve in desired or unwanted experiences. The one whose mind is calm and organized, utilizes conducive as well as non-conducive types of situations in an advantageous way because he looks at them unattached."

Generally the average income of the people keeps on increasing but contentment, harmony, complacency, joy and quiescence remain almost at the same level; this is a strange fact!.

Then, where should we search for harmony and happiness? The wise ancients have studied, in depth, the nature of man and concluded that beside exuberance and accumulation of material super-abundance, if other spheres, or circles of life could be fulfilled, the altitude of satisfaction and serenity may attain greater heights.

These newer circles of life have strength, power, beatitude and all-round progression. The person who strives for noble deeds and performs skillfully cannot commit sin.

Let us ponder upon some techniques which are useful, worldly-smart and aid to polishing our individuality:

Increase knowledge, perception and cognizance continuously: This achievement could be attained by study, sharp observation and company of the learned.

Don't be narrow-minded: It is possible only by open-minded, compassionate and scientific approach. By efforts we can rise above the level of fanaticism, caste and colour taboo, and societal discrimination. By doing these experiments you can pull down the walls of guilt which restrict and confine your personality.

Develop originality, practicality and general awareness in thoughts: Be aware about fresh thinking and possibilities of newness in every action. The social, personal and emotional intelligence evolves in the media of total awareness. Alert, awake, energetic, dynamic you!

Don't leave companionship of diligence and honesty: Having patience to work rightly, quality of reliability, refuge in the purity of heart and human values, compassion, love, judicious human relationship – to acquire all these noble traits, one has to deliberately work hard; such attempts may make your existence a calm, loving, balanced and benevolent phenomenon.

Let the grace of heart bloom: Forgiveness and amnesty generate such a serenity of mind which one does not get from material comforts. Firm faith in divine power and universal spirituality, hopefulness in heart, and optimistic thought-flow are the highways for travelling to reach the 'destination fulfillment', which normally one does not acquire only by redundant prosperity.

Enthusiasm, pleasantness of mind, and light-heartedness: One must try rearing and caring for these positives in life. Work, we have to; then why not be enthusiastic about it? Why with a long face? Whichever challenge comes forth, use smooth, rhythmic attitude to meet it. Beside this, look for the lighter and gay facet of life; most of the happenings are ludicrous as they cause laughter. Not many incidents are worth taking to the heart as extra luggage. Therefore, smile, laugh, and indulge in hearty laughter; enjoy the elixir of cheerfulness and glee. While walking on these paths, you can never commit ignoble, despicable *karma*.

Happiness, Karma and Fruition of Karma:

Money is necessary for purchasing things, as it has purchasing power, but it is not necessary that fabulous money may make one happy, because money is not abstract like happiness. Such contradiction appears to be unbelievable – i.e., the more our purchasing power increases (excellent food, elegant clothing, residence and other things of comfort), the higher becomes the degree of our depression, loneliness, emptiness, lowness of spirit, and a feeling of futility of life, a vacuum, a void, a vague sense of loss!

Do you know why it happens? It happens because we always act with a selfish attitude; only for us and our family; we never reflect upon to lessen a bit of pains and sorrows of the world. We always think about our own comfort, enjoyment, name and fame. All the more, even while praying to the deity, we beg for our own profit and desire fulfillment.

But it must be taken for granted that we can't raise the level of our pleasure and peace unless we connect ourselves with meditation, knowledge of truth, selfless service to others, *Ātman*, kindness, charity towards destitute, and mental balance. By negativity in action we can never develop self-confidence and noble character. We must also understand that beyond the network of our safety and life-supportive systems, excessive money has little worth. The wealth is necessary, no doubt, but outside of the circumference of 'enough is enough' where our freedom falls in jeopardy, the value of money remains only in multiplying money itself.

Contrary to this, positivity in action and service to the society as well as Nature give birth to self-confidence, hope for future, peace and fearlessness, which remain supportive to us during bad times. These could prove to be more helpful than money, because they generate enormous energy in our mind to endure bashing of bad sectors during the journey of life.

The mental sufferings and upheavals can't be calmed down by means of wealth alone; for that a solid base of truthful character and the knowledge of reality are needed.

The cheerful and pleasant persons are generally healthy and survive longer than the depressed, dull ones. The wise people overflow with divine bliss, knowledge of the Self and humane emotions. They are not hungry amid the gluttony of prosperity.

Conclusion

Act vigorously to earn comfort, live the life joyfully, but at the same time recognize the values of noble karma. While performing action, have a longing for the reward of your hard labour, but don't crumble down and be disintegrated in the wild, dreadful desire for that reward. Let go all out for noble karma!

•

Resonance – 3

Karma is the cause of Universe:
The mother of joy and sorrows;
Life, death, then a sprout on Chakra,
Of yesterdays, to-days and tomorrows.

God is acting, though He's nothing to do,
Atom, cosmos, sun and moon –
All are moving across the time,
As is Karma so is the curse or boon.

A tiny creature, worm, or a whale-
Searching pleasure, night and day,
Creation's crown, the 'clever' man –
Longs for infinite joy to stay!

Man thinks not – 'good or bad'?
Where is the bliss? Known to rare,
Swimming in sludge of sensuous craze,
Hells beckon, a few are aware!

All is changing, a spin of wheel,
Dancing fancies, varied in kind,
How can one be full and filled?
How to enrich the ego and mind?

Know that all are free to act,
Gather the grains, or the husk,
Paint a rainbow in the life,
Acts will make it dawn or dusk.

End of the show dissolves our brain,
Yet the vibrating quanta of thought,
Travel beyond the live-show,
Mind never dies, and decays not!

Mind, if focused on the Truth –
Karma can never chase or hunt,
If we surrender unto His feet –
Sins of Karma are roasted, burnt!

Leaving the dreaded sultry gloom,
Let us walk towards Light,
Expand the heart, spread the wings!
Get up! Fly! It's the end of night!

Calm and simple, serene and joyous
Laughing and singing, pilgrims we,
Dance as karma with hope and faith
Realize and fly with/ towards Him! Free!

•

Take in a Stride – 3

Pay attention to impermanence of all things, situations and systems of the world.

Environments of your existence go on changing every moment. Adapt and adjust yourself accordingly, and with ease.

Every human being is born with innate wisdom; hence, throughout the life, he must continuously brighten it.

Normally, there is nothing in the world for which we should always lament and remorse.

Dissect and *analyze* the nature of your sufferings by your philosophy, methodology of Nature's action, awareness of your attachments, and sharp, piercing power of discrimination. Every day think about five blessings of your life which God has bestowed.

One has to do actions; then, why not to engage in such activities which brighten your individuality.

Earn wealth, live comfortably, and share your happiness with others in a suitable manner.

Look at the world intently; after certain level, the wealth cannot offer extra joy to you.

Clemencies, empathy, helping-hand to destitute; and serene contentment are the only path-ways, which lead to sunshine and bliss.

Every day, search for any one absurdity in the world and laugh heartily on that.

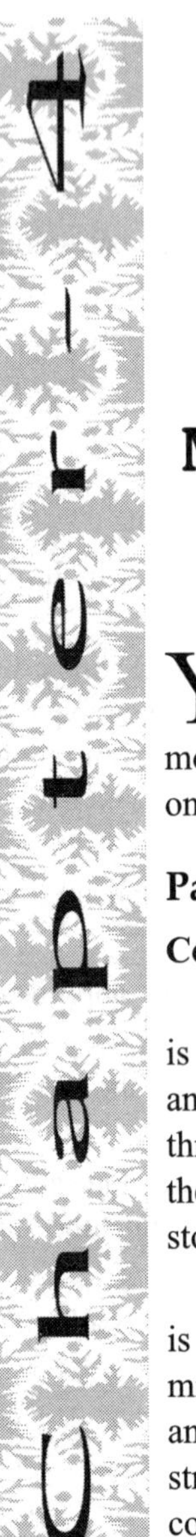

Meditation: The Gateway to Freedom

Yoga means to join; it's Spiritual unification. From amongst several methods, Yoga is the most important way by which man may become one with the Almighty.

Patanjala Yoga

Control of rising mental waves is Yoga

According of Maharishi Patanjali, our *Chitta* is constituted by three elements: mind, intellect and ego. The mind receives worldly experiences through senses; the intellect classifies them and then reacts; and the ego absorbs these stimuli and stores within.

Our *Ātman* (soul, Self, eternal consciousness) is beyond the reach of the waves which arise in our mind; therefore, unless we control these vibrations and disturbances of mind, or even understand their structure, we cannot have a revelation of our Self; consequently, the God realization will remain an impossibility.

When, through the control of mental spirals, the mind becomes tranquil and uncontaminated, the being comes face to face with own real nature. In other words, at this stage of attainment, the *Sādhaka* (the practitioner, the seeker) discards away his name, passion towards body, egotism, fame, etc., because all of them are mortal and impermanent. Thus opines Maharishi Patanjali.

Patanjali is the ancient doyen of the wise, the most experienced and respected, who formulated Meditation (*Dhyān Yoga*) centuries ago. He laid down simple and brief formula encompassing this complex subject. Although the original sources of the concept of meditation are *Upanishads* and *Gitā*, it was he who made this celestial knowledge available to the masses in an explicit meaningful way.

It has been declared, "Until the seeker does not get established in the yogic trance, he perceives his own nature just as the thought-waves project out. There are five types of *Chittavriti* (thought wave circles): real knowledge, false knowledge, confusion, sleep (ignorance), and memory. One can check and streamline these tendencies of thoughts by practice and renunciation. The renunciation is that state of mind where one abandons greed and hankering for worldly allurement, and the aspirant gets freedom from desires."

The yoga of meditation comes to fulfillment and completion by monitoring the thought waves and concentration; and one achieves concentration under the light of faith, energy, awareness, absorption (*Samādhi*) and prudence. *'Om'* (sound echoing as *Aum*) is the echo vibrating from the Omnipotent energy of the creator. By contemplating on the resounding *'Om'*, the revelation of *Ātman* comes forth and all obstacles on the path of true knowledge are destroyed.

For those, most of us, who live in the ups-and-downs of the world, Patanjali advises: by extending a hand of friendship towards the happy persons, by showing kindness towards downtrodden, by expression of pleasantness towards virtuous persons, and by remaining indifferent to the wicked, one may achieve stable peace of mind.

Beside these, Maharishi shows certain methods which could be helpful in attaining *tranquility* and concentration:

To repeatedly exhale and then keep the breath outside, as long as it is comfortable to do so,

To focus the mind at a 'spot of light' within,

To visualize a detached sage or mahātmā,

To think about a gracious, heavenly scene of a dream,

To create a ripple-less state of mind as if in deep sleep, and

To concentrate upon own ideal deity.

By practice, the mind surrenders and remains under control. When all the circles of mental waves come to stand still, the mind gets in union with the ultimate light. It dissolves in, merges with, and joins its source. This state is called *Samādhi* (absorption).

At this stage, the knowledge of the aspirant fills up to the brim with the brilliance of the Truth which is the highest altitude of enlightenment: the knower of all knowledge.

In this manner, all the *karma*, mental engravings and tendencies are cleaned and washed off.

It is further narrated: *Tapa*, study of scripture and surrender of action's reward at the altar of the Almighty, make the first step of *Kriyāyoga* (methodical approach to meditation by way of action).

By this technique, we can generate the energy of concentration and remove the obstacles which stand lofty on the way through which path the Light of Cosmic Intelligence descends upon our being. In actuality, these obstacles are the root cause of our sufferings and sorrows. Such hurdles, in assembly, consist of: darkness of ignorance, egotism, passion, hatred, jealousy and a wild desire to remain alive for ever (*abhinivesh*), or in other words 'the fear of death'.

As a matter of fact, it is the ignorance, or lack of knowledge (*Agyān*) about the reality, which blocks all the roads to revelation. These *tobula rosa*, the dark nights or conflicts, are:

To understand the impermanent as infinitely permanent phenomenon,

To consider the pain-givers as pleasant, and

To take unreality as reality.

This is that *Agyān* which ignites the tsunami-like tornado in our mind. However, we can annihilate these causes by meditation.

The experiences of pleasure and pain are the result of our noble and ignoble deeds, respectively. At this juncture it is important to note that spiritually awakened persons take all experiences as troublesome; both pleasant as well as unpleasant ones because the pleasant state of affair is also momentary and doomed to be lost.

It is further said that the suffering of the future times could be softened if we stop agitating about the reward of today's *karma*.

- When the whole being starts practising: discernment and acute awareness, then the self, advances towards freedom.
- When the ignorance is washed off completely, the causal factors of *Klesha* also get destroyed, and the seeker becomes free from the bondages of *karma*.

- Our *Ātman* shines forth in its brightest nature! This is *Moksha, Nirvana,* liberation.
- *Shwetashwatropnishad* is clear about it: "*Ātman is subtler than the subtle and grosser than the gross; his abode is the heart of all beings. By the grace of the Almighty if someone realizes the Ātman, and sees the Supreme in its glow, such a person gets rid of all sufferings.*"

The pathway of meditation (*Dhyānyoga*) founded by Patanjali is very comprehensive; it includes practice of *Prānāyām* (systematic breathing), *Dhārnā*, (fixing the mind on to the object of concentration) *Dhyān* (to hold the mind on the object of meditation) and *Samādhi* (when the object alone shines); also, the varied nature of power and faculties which an aspirant receives as he progresses in *Sādhnā* (practice of devotion) have been elaborated by Patanjali; but it has been warned that the seeker must not get entangled into the allurement of these powers, else all may go waste. Hence, it has been advised that the achiever of extraordinary powers must abandon their attraction so forth.

In the end, all sorrows, pains and upheavals of the mind come to a silence and the *Chitta* completely dissolves into the Infinite.

For us, the worldly people, it would be appropriate if we follow only some of these directives, to start with, the restless state of our mind could be tranquilized, and then a lasting happiness may prevail.

In our day-to-day experience we may decipher the meaning of these teachings that there are two main factors: discriminative intellect (*Viveka*) and offering of the reward of our actions at the holy feet of the God.

Viveka

The extended purport of *Viveka* is to recognize good and evil, to differentiate truth from untruth, to identify illusion from reality, to diagnose the true nature of life-death, pain-pleasure, ups-and-downs and all such contradictory duos, and in the end, against the cosmic backdrop of the Lord and the nature to realize every moment the flow of deep silence of mind, bliss, and love within. The second element is – dedication of the outcome or the result of our action to the God: involve in work dexterously, diligently, systematically, keeping the objective in sight, and also having a longing for achieving that goal. If we lose the interest in the result of our toil, we may also lose the interest in doing hard labour; yet there must not be any fear, anxiety, greed or agitation about success or non-success.

If we offer every aspect of *Purusārtha* to the Supreme, then from where the apprehension and fearfulness will thrive? The future, fate or destiny, spheres of prosperity, change in routes of life's journey; all are veiled under the cover of probability. These descriptive terminologies are varied names of the Cosmic Energy. Nobody can ever decipher them. Then, why to worry about the fruits of our actions? Yet, strive hard in doing righteous *karma*, remain established in *Dhyānayoga*, pay homage of acquirements to the omnipotent, and clasp success and non-success in your arms smilingly. While doing your duty, whatever comes to you as its result is His grace; accept it as His endowment and gift to you. Then and then only one may live happily, else suffers all the time – even he possesses redundant luxury.

Earn prosperity, live comfortably, help the destitute, and indulge in great laughter! Look at the convulsive and tremulous state of mind and the absurdity of jumping the humans do; and then smile!

The Path of the Zen

More than two thousand and five hundred years ago, Buddhism originated as a branch of Hinduism. Through centuries, Buddhism spread far and wide in the east and south-east Asia. In a new environment, novel techniques were evolved within the yogic system, but still the fundamental basic structure of yoga remained unaltered.

Dhyān (meditation) is called '*Chan*' in Chinese language and 'Zen' in Japanese. The philosophy of Zen is also erected on the – 'Base of unison' or 'centrality of awareness'. Such centering of alertness is pin-pointed upon the 'Eternal Present' only, not on the past, not on the future! To focus the mind or awareness on the present also means that the *Sādhaka* should try to attain a state where the knower, the knowledge and the known unify into one; there remains no distinction amongst these entities. This practice, ultimately transforms into the *Samādhi*.

In the disciplined exercise of Zen, it is an assurance that the enlightenment may descend suddenly in a flash, in our being. Awakening is a natural phenomenon and an intelligible experience which shines forth at the blink of eye-lid. Also, the methodology of Zen is straight, simple and non-spiraling. Answers to very complex questions are found in the practical living system of day-to-day life; for example, 'What is religion? Answer to this question is – 'Today is fine weather'. Apparently this is an absurdity, but in actuality it is an attempt to dislodge the mind from beaten track or ordinary habit of stale thinking pattern. This exercise makes the *Chitta* clean and innocent.

According to the Zen philosophy, the nature of our mind is basically uncontaminated and unstained hence attempts to clean it introduce newer kind of dirt into it. The real mind is a non-mind; the original *Chitta* is an *achitta*. The freedom from mind is the highest cleanliness. By artificial or prescribed discipline, our mind can never become a 'free mind'. In other words, if we can perceive the structure and organization of our mind, and if we are able to 'watch' the mind under the light of awareness, the immaculate and unadulterated, pristine nature of the mind shines forth. Let the row of thoughts come in, and let them go but remain alert and aware. Don't try to crush your thoughts, don't hinder, or interfere, neither to catch nor to stop them. Let them fade out themselves.

The modern Zen has evolved after passing through diverse channels of evolution; the new Zen emphasizes more upon the practicality of concept rather than its theoretical aspect. In this respect, Zen and *Karmayoga* come to stand side by side. Go on performing simple, seemingly ordinary actions, and you will attain Zen. This is the main conviction.

Beside this, other teachings of Zen are:

Not to live in a negative indifference towards the world,

To have a knowledge of cosmic illusion, that is –cognizance of the truth of mortality,

To accept that along with good things and happiness, there also exist bad things and unhappiness,

All situations are relative; not infinite, absolute, determinate or ascertained,

None of the situations, conducive to pleasure, remains as such forever,

Life and death are the locations or levels of the time, not radical change or violent break-up,

Watch the flow of happenings, without blocking; the time will come to a standstill,

The past as well as the future has no existence,

The one who can't live delightedly in the present, can never be happy anywhere,

Zen is not a practice of self-elevation because the human is fundamentally a custodian of divinity,

The Reality is 'as it is': the Such-ness, the Truth, the Existence,

Nothing is troublesome, nothing is amiable; 'what it is, so is it.'

The Truth or Reality is our nature: Beyond words, and

The Existence of Reality is 'Emptiness and Void'.

But it is not 'Empty' literally. Yet, if we chase the mirage in a desert, we get hold of only 'emptiness!'

These are some of the *sutras* (formulas) of Zen philosophy.

The essence of Zen is: continual involvement in action, no agitation about the reward of your action, and not to search for a direct meaning of any spiritual truth. Don't pollute your mind, on and on, by untried and untested answers.

The processes of Zen yoga are very extensive and matter of suggestive interpretation hence we shall further contemplate on it.

Simple, spontaneous or natural *karma* is thought to be the highest grade action; the action undertaken in the shadow of uncertainty or prolonged meandering analysis is considered as unnatural.

This means – our intellect must not split or get divided while working in the world; a mind under the influence of doubt remains entangled in the cob-web of alternatives, and in the trembling balance. One decision, one focus, one determination! When a person thinks too much to take the first step for acting, or he is over-conscious to decide about it, he can't begin his task in time. Under the pressure of intensive contradictions, incertitude and hesitation, the mind stumbles. Therefore, Zen opines: 'when you have to walk, then keep on walking; when sitting, keep sitting; but it is most necessary not to be on the horns of a dilemma; not to hesitate!'

In this way, the emphasis of Zen is more on activity rather than on mere thinking about it. Whatever challenge you face, and whichever direction of action you think to be the most suitable, start working to meet it without being in a fix. This is Zen. This approach is possible when we remove the hurdles which arise in the mind and block our way to act. Not to get stuck-up in any situation.

There is no 'aim' or objective of the Zen practice – such as, to receive enlightenment or *Nirvāna.* If one determines a purpose for Zen practice then Zen loses its innate essence. And when there remains no plan to achieve a target, then Zen transforms into a divine bliss: a Dynamic Present Moment!

Let us now ponder upon other spheres of Buddhism:

- To recognize untruth is the real knowledge or 'awakening'.
- Because of hassles in life, we do not pay attention to the beatitude around us.
- The style of action in Zen yoga is directed by our determination.
- Whatever we have to do, we must get involved in it, fully and totally.
- The complex systems within our body, which keep us throbbing, also work without hesitation.
- Our dynamic thoughts also germinate from the field of intuition.
- Hence, to do actions, without getting entrapped in the mire of alternatives is called Zen.

- Cleansing of the hurdles erected by doubts, fear and wild desires is known as Zen yoga.

Besides these dimensions of the cognizance, to be seated in a posture (*Āasana*), with stable mind, without fluctuating, and to meditate make a higher state of 'practice' but during such meditation no figure, form, sound or conviction is opted as an object or aim for attainment. Only, to sit comfortably on the seat, with folded legs, and not to 'do' anything, not even to blockade the thoughts.

In whichever methodology or philosophy we might believe, it is certain that the elements of Zen yoga can remove our sufferings.

"Whatever is – it is"; Why to struggle against the facts of life?

Beside the Zen, the Buddhist Philosophy includes 'mindfulness' (*Manoyoga*) and 'Single-pointed-ness of the mind (*Ekagrachittatā*) in meditation'. In mindfulness, one has to keep unbroken meditative awareness upon the 'Present moments' of one's life. To concentrate, with alertness, upon total sensitivity of senses and on all thoughts arising from the mind is 'mindfulness'. If we are unable to calm down the gushing flow of thoughts, at least we can stand apart and away from them looking from a distance; we can break our relationship and intimacy with our thought-current, in the least. It also means: to feel or to 'listen' attentively to all the experiences of the current time, i.e., the present moments. *Prānāyām* is an effective technique to achieve this goal.

The breathing regulatory exercise in Zen is also a simple and facile technique. The breathing is not stopped deliberately. Only in a natural way, the air is inhaled, then without holding forcefully it is exhaled gently but while exhaling it has to be pushed a bit farther with effort; then let the breath come in by inhalation. This is the Zen *Prānayam*.

If we focus our thoughts on the deep sense and feelings of joy and pleasant state, all desires, worries and fears may disappear. If our mind achieves a state of happiness in continuity, our thought may then be controlled effectively: a practice to live in ecstasy balance and rhythm in life.

And in the end, the state of ecstasy also vanishes; then, only the awareness of existence continues to shine in our life. This is *Samādhi* (absorpsion). On this pathway, the infinity of the Absolute Truth comes in the range of our vision. Total 'emptiness', 'void' or 'nothingness' extends and expands unimaginably; the grandeur of pure light of revelation descends in our being. This is the consummation of the meditative concentration.

Meditation in the *Gitā*

Yoga is the field of extensive knowledge. From amongst several paths, *Rājyoga* is such a *Sādhnā* through which all the dimensions of human personality can be evolved. It mainly consists of training of the *Chitta* (mind, ego, intellect, etc., inclusive) and the *will power* which extends a possibility of their all-round development. The meditation is an integeral element of the *Rājyoga*. The aim of yoga, including meditation, is to annihilate those hindrances which hold-up the mind from dissolution with the Cosmic Awareness.

One can attain acute focus of mind and also steer the tendency of desires towards the ultimate aim, by travelling on the highway of meditation.

The *Rājyoga* is founded on the psychological principle that if the mind, intellect and ego (whole *Chitta*) of man are impure, they clutch him in bondage of desires and sensuality; that means, he cannot breathe in un-interrupted freedom. It sounds a contradictory statement that only the disciplined *chitta* is able to make the man free from clutches of slavery. Obviously, only that *chitta* can lead you to enlightenment which has been cleansed by self-realization.

These principles mean – The knowledge is essential to perceive your own Self, and to beget knowledge it is urgent to eradicate the obstacles which create hurdles on the way of *Sādhnā*. This can be achieved only by meditation.

The *Rājyoga* is also known as *Ashtāngyoga*

(Yoga with eight appendages, strata)

Yama - Non-violence, truthfulness, non- stealing, continence, non-covetousness,

Niyama - Cleanliness, Non-contentment, austerity, study and contemplation, faith in the Almighty,

Āasana - Lotus posture, comfortable posture, etc., that makes the body steady,

Prānāyāma - To regulate and to take rhythmical breathing,

Pratyāhāra - To monitor the sense organs suitably, and then turning the organs inwards,

Dhārnā - To concentrate upon our ideal,

Dhyāna (meditation) - In transcendental state to focus upon the *Ātman* – beyond the circle of mind,

Samādhi - Dissolution of all conflicts, end of knower, knowledge and the known.

All of these eight strata are to be perfected for attaining a higher state of consciousness. *Dhyāna,* the seventh rug of the stair, is known as meditation. *Dhyānyoga* is a simple and easy process, but before that the first six steps are compulsory to be crossed so that the mind becomes stainless, the body remains balanced in fitness, the desires do not go haywire, and the tendencies be regulated. Then only one can succeed in *Dhyānayoga,* else not.

Dynamic Awareness

How does meditation help the aspirant to attain Dynamic Awareness?

To this reference *Gitā* declares:

या निशा सर्वभूतानां तस्यां जागर्ति संयमी।
यस्यां जाग्रति भूतानि सा निशा पश्यतो मुनेः।।

(2:69)

That which is night to all beings, in that the self-controlled man keeps awake; where all beings are awake, that is the night for the Sage; who sees.

In this *Shloka*, the night metaphorically represents the ignorance about the truth because the brilliance of the Self *(Ātman)* remains veiled for the unaware, unconscious person. The other aspect of interpretation is that most of the mundane, worldly people remain sunken in sensuality and greed; on the contrary, the yogi keeps standing apart with an attitude of indifference towards these allurements, he sleeps on towards animal pleasure and hedonism.

The one who is arrogant, convoluting in the sludge of bodily pleasure, having closed and stale thinking, generally avoids the path of divine bliss and enlightenment; and the awakened, knowledgeable person does not get attracted towards the glitter of luxuriant traps in the world.

This attitude of the yogi takes him into the realm of Dynamic Silence:

बाह्यस्पर्शेष्वसक्तात्मा विन्दत्यात्मनि यत्सुखम्।
स ब्रह्मयोगयुक्तात्मा सुखमक्षयमश्नुते।।

(5:21)

With the self unattached to the contacts outside, he finds happiness in the Self; with the self-engaged in the meditation of Brahman, he attains endless happiness.

Renunciation (dispassion, non-attachment) has been considered by the wise to be the highest form of happiness. They opine that such *Ānanda* is immutable, permanent; not the sensual pleasure. It also connotes that if we dump the negativity of the world, we may make an entry into the sphere of positivity. Then, we recognize the dynamic aspect of our individuality.

Who is a Yogi?

Further, characteristics of a Yogi are enumerated:

योऽन्तःसुखोऽन्तरारामस्तथान्तर्ज्योतिरेव यः।
स योगी ब्रह्मनिर्वाणं ब्रह्मभूतोऽधिगच्छति॥

(5:24)

He who is happy within, who rejoices within, who is illuminated within, that yogi attains Absolute freedom, and becomes Brahman himself.

Who can attain the *Brahman*, the Absolute? The question pops up……!

The aspirant, who seeks dispassion, gets himself detached from the absurdity of the external feast for senses, and thus he finds the internal bliss. This is the attainment of the Absolute.

Gitā also lays down certain methods, in brief, for concentration: by mentally severing the contact of senses with the outer world; by focusing eyes, half or fully closed, at the centre of eyebrows (conceptual focus), then regulating inhaling and exhaling breathe.

That way, monitoring the 'movement' of senses, mind and intellect, and merging the Self with the highest Ideal: freeing from desires, fear and anger are essential. One, who adopts meditation earnestly, undergoes a transformation to become a free person.

Other particulars of a Yogi are: that the yogis are Self-disciplined; calm and cool; balanced in conflicting situations; and contended with *Gyān* and prudence. They are: custodians of un-quivering intelligence, winners over desires and are free from passion and hatred.

Ways of Meditation

These are the symbolic indicators; the one who becomes adept in the conceptual essence of these gems of wisdom, enters the *Nirvikalpa Samādhi;* absorption in totality.

The *Gitā* also chalks out practical techniques to conduct meditation:

- Be seated in a clean place, on a stable platform which is neither very high nor too low.
- Concentrate the mind on one 'point'; organize the activities of the mind.
- Cleanse the mind, remove the clutter.
- Remain unmoved in lotus posture; keep head, neck and torso or trunk of the body straight; focus the 'sight' of the mind on the tip of the nose; don't look anywhere; close the eyes softly and lightly.
- Remain pleasant, fearless; control the waves of mind which may continuously arise to disrupt; visualize your *Istadev* (ideal), sound, shape, with or without form, or symbol of any other divine power-centre. While passing thorough this phase, slowly merge with the highest object of your aspiration, remaining in deep contemplative state at least half an hour in the early morning and also for the same period in the evening.

The Results

The Yogi who keeps his mind in stark balance gets established in the eternal peace of the *Brahman*.

The seeker who commands, regulates, or takes the middle path (i.e. not the extreme) in his eating, enjoyment, duty, hard labour, sleeping or in being awake, all his *klesha* (troubles) come to an end by way of Yoga.

At the time of merger with the Self, the *Chitta* (mental manifestations) of the yogi stabilizes firmly like flame of an earthen lamp in a place where there is no breeze.

By following these ways, the tsunami upheavals of our mind can be subsided by meditation.

When by practice of Yoga, the mind reaches the state of *tranquility* and peace, and the *Sādhaka* gets connected with the Self, then the yogi directly experiences the infinite ecstasy, which transcends the experience of senses and the mind, then the aspirant receives immutable brilliance of the Truth. After being bestowed upon by all this bliss, the Yogi realizes that nothing is left which could be better than this experience to achieve. Thereafter, the blessed Yogi never gets upset or agitated, even at the time of immense sufferings and sorrows. To be free from *Klesha* is the culmination of achievement through Yoga.

In the rhythmic symphony of meditation, the devotee sees the presence of energy of the Self in all beings of the world and also the presence of total existence in his own *Ātman;* it means, for him there is none who is low or high in status of any sort. Therefore, in joy or sorrow, he never gets upset.

It is a conviction in the Hinduism that at the time of leaving this body if the dying one visualizes any creature or human being, he takes his next birth in that particular womb; by practising meditation throughout one's life, the mind of such a person could be fixed on the Almighty, hence at the time of grand departure it becomes easier to concentrate upon Him. With the result, the being easily merges with the infinite energy of the Creator.

The *Gitā* says:

प्रयाणकाले मनसाचलेन
भक्त्या युक्तो योगबलेन चैव।
भ्रुवोर्मध्ये प्राणमावेश्य सम्यक्
स तं परं पुरुषमुपैति दिव्यम्।।

(8:10)

At the time of death, with an unshaken mind full of devotion, by the power of yoga, fixing the whole breath (Prāna) between the two eyebrows, the devotee reaches the Supreme Purush having brilliant form.

Only the one who cognizes the infinite power of *Ishwara*, and experiences His manifestations all-through the cosmos, can totally imbibe the radiance of the yoga; and all the *Kleshas* of such a Yogi could be eradicated, even if there dances turmoil in the world.

With regard to *Dhyānyoga*, Sri Krishna promises that by walking on this path one is blessed with *Buddhiyoga* (unison with Cosmic Intelligence); the rise of pure consciousness. This is imminent: Awareness of intuition within!

The Almighty Brahman

In order to get established firmly in meditation, it is a must to understand – even as a flash of glimpse – the infinitude of God's Power, His omnipresence and Omni-pervasiveness, although no one can know that power in totality:

The abode of the God, the Almighty Brahman, is in the heart of all beings.

He is the Beginning, Middle and the End of all.

He is the causal seed of all elemental existence.

Without that energy nothing can exist.

His fire sparks in all movables and immovable.

Whatever is beautiful, grandeur, and prosperous, it is the expression of His Glory.

The universe functions by only a particle of His power.

The whole cosmos pulsates within that Supreme Lord.

Birth...Death...Birth... goes on and on in the movement of the wheel of time within the fold of the Cosmic Form of the Lord.

To such an unlimited, highest power, one who surrenders with faith and offers worship reaches on the peak of Yoga. All unhappiness could be annihilated by full accomplishment of Yoga:

ये तु सर्वाणि कर्माणि मयि संन्यस्य मत्पराः।
अनन्येनैव योगेन मां ध्यायन्त उपासते।।

(12:6)

But those who worship Me, renouncing all actions in Me, regarding Me as the Supreme Goal, meditating on Me with single minded devotion...

...For them whose minds are set on Me, O Partha! Verily I become soon the Saviour out of the ocean of finite experiences of the world.

By practice, ultimately, the energy of the Self begins to support the yogi and the sun of *Sāttvik* thoughts dawns upon him; then, where could suffering thrive?

Conditions for Success in Yoga

Again, expounding the ways to gain success in Yoga, it has been said that the person who cultivates following characteristics becomes skilled in meditation:

Fearlessness	Purity of heart	Readiness to learn
Discipline of senses	Generosity in giving	Abandonment
Study of scripture	Steadfastness	Non-violence
Complete Surrender	Calmness	Mental
Renunciation	Serenity	Politeness
Transparency in behaviour	Softness in behaviour	Firm determination
Radiance of personality	Forgiveness	Purity
Absence of jealousy	Absence of pride	Truth

However, it appears improbable to adopt all the virtues listed above; hence one should ponder upon them while in meditative state. At the time of deep silence of mind, and intent awareness, if we absorb even one factor of goodness, the other blessing may thereafter begin to pervade our being.

After reaching to the summit, what happens?

ब्रह्मभूतः प्रसन्नात्मा न शोचति न कांक्षति।
समः सर्वेषु भूतेषु मद्भक्तिं लभते पराम्।।

(18:54)

Attaining unison with Brahman, serene in the Self, he neither grieves nor desires, keeps equanimity towards all beings. He obtains a Supreme Devotion towards Me:

The Yogi is completely fulfilled in the Self, therefore he never feels sorry on facing sufferings. He has no feeling of emptiness, so he does not desire impermanent satisfaction and sensuous joy. He does not chase outer pleasures because his Self-pleasure fills up his being.

Such a calm and balanced seeker discovers own spring of bliss within, which is not controlled by any allurement of the material world. He continues to do actions as duties in the world but the values of life for him are different than other people. Thus, he always remains close to the Almighty.

•

Symphony – 4

Beside *Vedas, Upnishadas*, *Gitā*, Buddhism and their off-shoots: Tao, Zen; and Yoga Sutra of Patanjali, several other philosophers and theologists have proposed principles of meditation in varied ways. From amongst these, thoughts of Rene Descartes (1596-1650) are interesting. His book – 'Meditation' was published in 1641 AD in which there are certain comments on the basic questions on philosophy of meditation, differing from the tradition of meditation in India. We can't term Descartes' principles as *Dhyāna*, but we may call them 'Fields of deep contemplation'.

According to Descartes:

The essence of life factors must be *analyze*d on the basis of Skepticism or questioning; in other words, you should look at the 'so-called truths' with doubtful attitude. If some 'thinker' or knowledgeable person wishes to propose any principle in the field of *Gyāna* (Knowledge of the Truth), he must, first of all, cleanse his own mind by rubbing-off all prejudices, opinions, impressions, beliefs or inclinations. The learning and experiences which we acquire through our senses may also deceive us!

Descartes says: "I am – because I think. It means – I can have an insight about my soul only through the medium of thoughts. I am not the body."

The soul (Consciousness or *Ātman*) definitely exists – there is no doubt about it – but whether 'body is, or not' it remains questionable; therefore, the body and the soul should be thought of as separate entities.

If we perceive the world with pure mind, without conditioned thoughts or logic, we may be able to know the reality of the truth, mind, body, God, freedom, life and the world. Our discriminative insight, or ken (*Viveka*), can rip open the illusion of unreality.

We create paths of our life because of our longings to achieve the desired goal. In doing so, generally we neglect our original intuition or our conscience.

By analyzing the thoughts propounded by western thinkers it becomes clear that they are not as deep and sound as those of the eastern learning of the ancients.

In the western philosophical concepts, the practicality of theories remains a dominating factor, which merely reflects the materialistic views in their societies. Then, where is the capability to cognize the *Ātman*, or the God? Where is the tenderness of emotions arising in the human heart? How can they know the transcendental bliss of deep meditation? Because of this reason, the western concepts about spirituality appear as a system of arithmetic process, measurement or quantification, equation or mechanistic in form and organization.

But, the Bliss Absolute, the truth, the goodness, the beauty of truth transcend the logic, reason, physicality or worldly disposition of the mind. It is Trans-Time, Trans-all, what we perceive!

Awareness, Knower and Meditation

We may cognize our *Ātman* only by internal awareness, experiential acumen and deep natural intuition. This *Ātman* itself is the knower and also the Awareness. The meditation connects us with cosmic power; the waves of energy transform to project the vision of *Ishwara* in form before us. The grandeur, charm, shape, colour, form, characteristics, beatitude of such personal God (i.e. with form) spring forth from our own inclination and conviction about the divinity of our faith and mental disposition whether it is Sri Krishna, Shiva or Buddha – or any other centre of power, that which we are convinced about taking as our Ideal, *Ishta devta.* We can experience this revelation only by meditation which force changes the cosmic energy into the matter.

Sometimes, of course rarely, when the mind of a person becomes pure and clean, like that of a child – uncorrupt, on which no script has been engraved, and that which is overflowing with love, then at that flash of the moment, the energy of the Absolute sparks an intuiting instinct which takes the person into the realm of Truth; thus, enlightenment takes place instantaneously. This is the climax of meditation, culmination of Bliss, Ecstasy!

All 'things' of the universe are inter-connected because the energy exists in every atom, and the waves of the same energy fill the space which we erroneously call 'empty space'. Nothing is empty in the cosmos. All is completely filled with energy or its changed form, the matter. Our body is made up of atoms: Calcium, Hydrogen, Oxygen, Carbon, Iron, Potassium, sodium and atoms of several other elements.

Sand, soil, water, air, etc., all contain atoms and their particles, as their structure. Obviously, the living and non-living objects are connected with each other by the infinite energy wave. And every atom is the mother of enormous power like the power of the atom bomb! The cosmos is, in actuality, a thin membrane of energy on which all exists and remains interconnected.

Therefore, there is no difficulty in appreciating that in spite of distantly apart by time and space from each other, all things, happenings or situations are intertwined through the medium of the cosmic energy. The original fountain of that total energy always remains in contact with our *Chitti Shakti* or mental energy; one may tap that source whenever desire to do so. The quanta of your mental energy represent your Self and the eternal source of that infinite energy is the Almighty. The unison of these two phenomena is the yoga which can be consummated by way of meditation.

But to conceive this principle we must comprehend the whole existence, including ourselves, as one single formation in totality. We have to conceptualize the world, life, Nature, death, mind, God, *Ātman,* and all, together as a Cosmic Form (*Virāt Swaroop*), not in pieces, not as appendages, not as divisions. It is like loving a child as in wholeness, its complete being, not its grace and beauty differently. My previous life (if you believe), my coming into the womb of my mother, then birth, thoughts, life, relationships, ego, old age, death, rebirth (if you believe!), God, Universe, and in the backdrop of all uninterrupted, infinite, immutable, indestructible, non-altering awareness, dynamic power which goes on painting all on an infinitely gross canvas – all this functions as a 'completion' or an 'integrity'.

On that cosmic painting, I am a tiny dot, finer than a particle of the atom, a micro-entity to which no significance could be attached in the vastness of time and space; a nondescript existence! But, in spite of this scenario – 'I am', and I am important too, because I am an integral part of the vibrating painting on the cosmic canvas, and I am also existing within the grandeur and grace of that art. May be, I am a micro-minuscule dot, but I am!

Visualize! You are made up of only atoms, although they are somewhat compact at places to give you a shape, size and form. Think! All around you also, the particles emitted by atoms are shooting and floating with unimaginable speed in the ocean of energy. Meditate! The quanta of energy from your body, mind, intellect and ego are being dispersed; spreading with great force and velocity, and disseminating into the cosmic ocean of particles and energy wave. Your *Ātman* is watching all, enlightening the show, since the self is the infinite Light. Your existence merges within or absorbed by the cosmic energy. This is the highest goal of Yoga. This is the *Samādhi.*

Let us Find Answers

The great thinkers of the world generally opine in one voice that don't try to search answers to your questions on this matter. First of all, this remains a fact that most of such queries are basically incorrect – the questions which are asked concerning beings, world, *Ātman, Parmātman*, life, death, etc., because we put forth this inquisition from the confines or cage of our worldly experiences or applying intellect which is conditioned by our logic; we ask by taking a yardstick of 'cause and effect' which is again under a bondage of our thinking.

But, these cosmic and divine realms do not function by the force of your delimited 'reasoning' and experiences. They are metaphysical, transcendental, and beyond the logic of 'cause and effect'.

Then, what to do? How to quench the inquisitiveness of our mind, be it in bondage? If we don't find answers, where from and how to get peace and happiness?

According to Socrates – 'Don't hunt for answers in the past incidences, rather involve and keep busy your mind in some internal activity'. This statement means: 'Engage your thoughts in intellectual processing which can open the gate of true knowledge, whether it solves your problems, or not.' In other words, the incidences of our past can never be true; that means, they can't be categorized as truth in the sense of the *truth of the life.*

It also connotes that if I search the answers by applying my intellect which is not free from previous conditionings, I may not be able even to touch the free truth. Hence, I remain an ignorant on this path.

Founded on the concept of Buddhism, 'Koan' is a technique in Zen for asking questions which are not straight; either the questions are self-contradictory or obviously uncertain so that the possibility of answering remains open-ended. Because of this state, Koan ultimately enters a 'Dynamic Void', where all is 'silence in live awareness'. We may be astonished to know that within an atom, which is a unit of Nature, there exists only 'silence'! This is the 'golden silence' of Buddha, *Neti-Neti* (not this., not this) of Vedas, 'ignorance' of Socrates, emptiness of Jesus, smile of Maharishi Raman, and 'the present is the only time' of Jiddu Krishnamurti. This is the emptiness of Alertness.

This is Yoga. This is *Dhārnā*, *Dhyāna Samādhi:* the methodology to make our mind an innocent, uncontaminated, unstained, transparent supporter of our Self so that the reflection of the infinite energy shines forth within our being.

Characteristics of success in Dhyāna Yoga

We can't say, if one day the populace of the world may take up Yoga on regular basis, then the violence, sufferings, pains, corruption, wars, hatred, poverty, disease and ignorance could be eradicated from the earth! Also, we do not know the percentage of people on the globe which practices Yoga and meditation and in actuality how many persons understand this wisdom of spirituality. This is also difficult to predict that every seeker may get a boon of revelation of the truth, and then by the grace of the God, all desires of human beings will be fulfilled and all natural calamities: such as, tsunami, earth-quakes, epidemics, mishaps, etc., will not occur at all on the earth!

But we know that the poisonous stings of negativity get subdued and their trauma lessened because of the positive energy created by those seekers who are committed to Yoga? Such 'Sages' sustain and support the world.

Characteristics of a Yogi

Who are such Yogis? Active sports persons, devoted scientists, artists, musicians, writers, teachers, students, doctors, engineers, computer experts, social workers, pilots, defense personnel, organizers, planners and people of several other categories who are engaged in creative activities with honesty and dexterity, and are trying to bring a little bit of happiness in the lives of others. They are all yogis of high achievement. No one can attain a success worth narration without *Dhyān Yoga*. Those who work with full concentration and potentiality perform their duty skillfully and also help a little to the destitute are all yogis; the followers of contemplative meditation.

The one who abandons the habit of utilizing one's past experiences in exploring the newer experiences, and the one who is aware that every moment the world of our knowledge is being created afresh and anew – that person is a wise being. The beauty of the mind of such a person lies in thc way he *analyzes*, with a fresh outlook, the ever-changing panorama of the world. This also means: *Be alert towards ever-flowing novelty and altering situations with calm and free mind! Remain awake, because unawareness is nothing but sleep*!

The *Dhyān Yoga* is a means to open up our own mind before us; else, normally we are unable to perceive the ups-and-downs, upheavals, dirt, wild longings and sensuous passion which lie hidden in the depth of our mind. The compact yet forceful desires, in due course of time, at a weaker moment, erupt out like a volcano and blast our *tranquility*. However, in deep meditation we are able to 'touch' the core of our Self, the consciousness. This energy of wisdom is present, in all sentient as well as non-sentient. The *Upanishada* calls it *'Ātman'* and the famous psychologist Jung names this spark as 'collective consciousness'; and the atomic physicists designate this power as 'Energy wave' or 'quanta'.

This is the only energy, power or 'cosmic glow' which could as well be called the 'Radiance of the *Ātmā*'. Meditation escorts us gently up to this Absolute divine light. We call it 'self-realization', enlightenment, or revelation of *Shakti*.

In addition to the enlisted virtues of Yogi, here are some more specialties of an adept Yogi:

A Yogi holds positive view-points towards the world; abides by the tried-and-tested values of life; possesses a righteous mind set; shows pleasing behaviour; is always fit and alert; believes in optimism; enjoys freedom from fear of death; explores total potentiality to achieve success; shows happiness, serenity and enthusiasm and unison with the cosmic intelligence.

If one practices meditation, these gems-of-grace begin to glitter in his/ her life. Then, nothing remains to be attained anymore.

How Can the Mind Know the Secret of 'Mind'?

Only through meditation.

Every person possesses a distinctive personality. This is a mental system on the basis of which the humans are capable of adapting to the ever-changing conditions of the world. According to Sigmund Freud, most of the mental world of the man remains active at the unconscious level of the mind from where the behaviour of a person is determined. The activities of the unconscious stratum remain a secret; from there the conscious mind receives strength or motivation for activities in the fields of experiences, emotions, and behaviour. But awareness about varied situations, common sense, beliefs and other thoughts are present at the conscious level. The unconscious mind only goes on instigating.

The basic instinct which arises from the unconscious mind always tries to control and dominate the conscious mind. The waves of instincts give birth to worry, sensuality, fear of death, wild desires, tension, feeling of happiness or unhappiness, etc. Normally our conscious mind is incapable of knowing its own unconscious layers wherein frustrations, hankerings, yearnings, penchants and acute longings continuously dance. These monsters suddenly, without warning, raise their heads and arise to the lofty heights; these are the causes of our *kleshas*, sorrows, pains, depression, and unhappiness.

Our thoughts and emotions take birth in the conscious mind because of the incoming reactions with the world through our sense organs. These experiences get deposited, one by one, and are locked in the castle of unconscious mind. The conscious and unconscious minds are separated from each other by a very strong wall therefore we can never know the subversive activity going on in the unconscious mind. But, this wall could be pulled down by the practice of concentration which could be reinforced through meditation, contemplation or any other similar procedure. Thereafter, one-by-one, the knots of unconscious mind get untied and we are shocked to see the heaps of sludge and filth within us. But this exposition and then the cleansing can be done only in the state of deep meditation. In this way our conscious mind can know the secret of our unconscious 'mind'.

Conclusions by Psycho-analysts

The symptoms of mental illness are like entangled knots, the causes of which take birth in the past and the present. For diagnosis of the disease, the patient is laid down on the bed, and asked to relax completely. Then he is asked to close his eyes and then narrate whatever comes to his mind.

By this technique, the mental figures of the patient are projected which indicate the condition of his mind. By this method, the unconscious mind of the person could be transformed into the conscious mind so that the strength of unconscious mind could be weakened; otherwise, using this strength, it goes on distorting the reality of life – i.e., it twists or deforms the truth and makes the person mentally ill.

But the psychological analysis cannot comprehend complete personality of a person. And the flowing influence of energy in between the ego, the thoughts in the unconscious chamber, and the intellect cannot be deciphered by this technique of analysis.

This is the conclusion derived by other scientists on the psycho-analysis method of Freud.

Superiority of Dhyān *Yoga*

Clear as it is, the *Dhyān Yoga* is much superior to psycho-analysis in this respect, as it is a medium to contact directly with the Self by which all the knots get destroyed in a natural way.

By meditation, when the scum of the mind is cleaned, the mirror reflects our real individuality. We begin to cross all the four dimensions of time-space and ultimately merge with the Cosmic Awareness; there remains neither happiness nor unhappiness because in the infinite extension of the cosmic system both of these states carry no sense. *Dhyān* pacifies the tsunami tornado and restores peace as well as balance in life. After settling in the serenity, we enter the cognition that every trauma, catastrophe, disaster or misfortune – all is a part or element, of the infinitely vast universal system. The life is 'such' because all its components are 'such'. Accept this fact and then continue to act for solutions of problems.

Practicable Yoga-practice

Generally, the aforesaid wise teachings of the ancients appear to be a complex cobweb to the mundane persons who are clutched in the worldly affairs, struggling for bread-and-butter or wrestling with dap-to-day family problems. No doubt, they follow certain sayings of the wise but most of it passes above their heads. No time, no patience, no deep ken, and sometimes no definite, unshakable faith; then, what can the *Dhyān Yoga* do? It is O.K. we are O.K. as we are!' They think so.

This situation, at first glance, appears to be acceptable and logical, but everybody realizes that at whichever level one is standing today, it is always beneficial to evolve a bit at the higher strata. Otherwise, what difference remains between man and the dog!

Now, we shall try to simplify all doctrines which are apparently twisted and serpentine. We shall transform the theories into a palatable dish but their basics will remain the same. It could be a possible exercise.

Base of Meditation

We take it for granted that the world as well as our body is permanent, immutable, while they are all altering at every tick of time. Because of this fact we suffer, or jubilate even in the momentary pain or pleasure.

The chamber of unconscious mind in the deep, is overflowing with obnoxious clutter and smudge which, from time to time, projects out as thorny growth in the conscious mind. To see through such dark smoke, it is the *Dhyāna* which enables us to destroy the ignorance.

If once we identify our corrupt mind, and start a cleansing operation, then the flood of our sorrows and sufferings (*klesha*) begins to recede.

Only the meditation can make us to experience the 'Awareness of Nothingness' or 'Dynamic *Tranquility*' of our mind. Then, by adapting the same path we may achieve the unison with the immaculate Self.

Ishwara, God, the Absolute *Brahman*, or the 'Fountain of cosmic energy' is a silent, wave-less, stainless, energetic Void, or 'Awareness in Nothingness.'

If one is fully established in *Dhyāna,* which is possible only by continued practice and cultivation of virtues, the individuality and consciousness of the aspirant alters beyond recognition. The blessed one thus becomes large-hearted, undeviating, steadfast, luminously kindled, custodian of all-round fitness, contended and balanced.

Once the consciousness (*chetnā*) of a person gets altered – inside out and outside in – thereafter he, living in the world, continues to do actions skillfully – without anxiety and worries.

Simple Methodology of *Dhyānyoga*

The following variation of *Prānāyām* is a simple methodology of *Dhyān Yoga*:

Every day, in the evening as well as morning, be seated in an āsana (lotus or half-lotus posture), at a lonely place of the house, which should be dimly lighted.

Close your eyes softly; don't move any part of the body.

Watch your breathing, mentally; be aware of inhaling and exhaling – ten counts.

Visualize your ideal, Ishta Devtā, light spot, the sun, your fovourite short mantra, a sparking dot, particle, or any symbol of your faith and conviction. Concentrate upon any one!

Exhale and, without using force, let the breath go out a bit farther than the normal; then inhale in a natural way. Seven times.

'Look' carefully the gushing thoughts in the mind; only watch with full awareness; don't crush, check or resist them; only by 'seeing', the agitation of thoughts slows down.

Don't be scared by dirty thoughts; don't pay attention on them. Only 'see'. Say 'cut...cut...cut.., three times.

In due course of time, the practice may result into calmness and slowing of the thought-current.

Ultimately, you may attain that state of mind where neither ideal, nor self and not even thoughts appear on the screen. In spite of this, you remain alert, aware, energetic and dynamic internally. You are not caught up by sleep.

This is the pathway of *Dhāranā, Dhyān* and *Samādhi*. Beside this, generally you are neither required to know more nor to do more. But, of course, if you're an inquisitive aspirant or a curious seeker, study treatises of wisdom, learn from an adept, and evolve your own method. Keep the object well-defined and adapt to practical course of journey.

This will prove to be a boon for you. Your life will change. This is not a religion, nor a fanatic narrow lane. This is the universal truth.

If you cannot perceive the complex definitions of theoretical principles, don't be disappointed. You have to go on attempting to maintain your status of high achiever, in spite of struggling for survival in the world. Starting from today up to the infinite extension of the time, how could you remain in the higher sphere of enlightened being? This you have to decide; determine using your knowledge, experience and divine intuition. It is your life; it must be your decision!

•

Resonance – 4

A wave of thought becomes windy blow,
Yoga keeps it cool, calm, as breeze slow.

Till the currents of mind dance in a blaze,
My world dances on wild waves in a craze.

He who offers the self, Yoga brightens the one,
When the mind stills, abides in Him, desires none.

If we clean the mirror, then upon Him meditate –
In a wink the Grace reflects, love and peace radiate.

Time only remains forever, the body and mind are to go,
Energy of our life keeps pulsating by the Absolute's glow.

Act, act to awaken in the dawn of pure land,
Work in the flow of Nature, don't block the divine hand.

Act and meditate, think of the present – today!
Past are gone and future lies in an unseen bay.

Others may sleep, be awake, and alert!
Be in *dhyān* when others play in sensuous dirt.

Work hard to prosper, remain virtuous, rise high,
Be a king and sage, be a free enlightened guy!

Know that 'you don't know', which is the real wisdom,
Show un-quivering faith in God, in inner Kingdom.

•

Take in a Stride – 4

Listen, read about spirituality but build your own philosophy.

Be convinced that if a man determines to accomplice any task, he can succeed in that; let the fate be seated at its proper place.

Every situation is a resultant effect of some cause which we know and also do not know; don't be over-excited to know the unknowable.

Nothing is superfluous in the world, therefore conserve and protect the environment.

Every day we go on approaching towards some grand goal of existence. Always be in search of that goal and remember the super organizer of the cosmic programme.

Nothing is totally bad; or completely good in this world. All is relative. To recognize is your prudence.

Nature is a Grand Cause and that cause is busy in some grand purpose; hence live in contact with Nature.

From time to time, *analyze* and cleanse your basic convictions, beliefs, opinions and experiences. It is not necessary that what we think is right.

Negate the modern conflicts and rigid materialism. Go on expanding the circumference of open-mindedness.

Continue to act; enjoy life fully; don't become miserable in absolute poverty; that means, earn solvency; and in the end, surrender all at the altar of the Cosmic Power, and attain Salvation (*Moksha*).

Pathways to Enlightenment

By walking on the 'Pathways of Enlightenment', we may perceive the Truth: a way to see the relationship between what we 'see,' and what is the 'reality' of the 'thing'. With reference to such a ken, we must understand that whatever we experience by means of our sense organs (and the mind), could be real and unreal as well. Then, how can we encounter that 'reality' which makes the current of energy to flow in the background of all actions, 'things' and incidences?

From time to time, the wise have shown us the way to overcome this difficulty: 'whatever you have accumulated and imbibed into your life so far, taking it for granted as 'truth'– rub it off to clean, and earn afresh!' This means, while living in the physical world, it is necessary to suitably organize our life; for this we need innumerable scientific and social facts, information and data about the world, which support our survival, progress and security. But, we have to bring several other aspects of our life into the fold of reassessment and rethinking;

such facts are related to our consciousness, our vital force of life; the maps or blueprints of these concepts have been engraved on our unconscious mind, right from the childhood. Such spheres of deep impressions are concerned with : Creation, soul, spirit, *Ātman*, divinity, spirituality, philosophy of life, life-death, present world-other world, *Karma*, *Dharma* or law of justice, and emotional experiences.

On the banner of every theory and metaphysical concept, stick a question mark of 'reason', logic and scientific evidences! Don't accept anything without getting satisfactory answer to your doubt. However, for such courageous steps, you must possess a treasure of knowledge prior to jumping into controversy. To have a vision of transparent, clear and pure truth is the ultimate aim of such logical analysis. Although the skeptical, intellectual and the cause-effect knives for dissection are also left behind because they in themselves can never reach up to the truth, yet they usher into the pathways of enlightenment.

An analytical approach to decipher the truth is an absurdity because such thoughts give birth to other thoughts and a vicious circle comes into motion. Thus, we can't reach anywhere. Hence, establish your own intuitive truth, translate it into experience and practical knowledge, and imbibe its energy into your life!

Brain and Mind

Our brain transmits stimuli to create our thoughts through billions of neurons (nerve cells). We continuously register our world in the brain through our sense organs. The world is as *it is* and we incessantly go on acting in that world. Either we take decision on various matters under the influence of our past experiences, or we choose one option out of several alternatives and work upon that one.

Are we *free* to act in the world, or does our fate steer our *karma* towards a predetermined target? The answer is not easy. If you accept that the fate or ultimate destiny is the monitor of all actions, then you lose your freedom to act. But, if you want to save your freedom of action, then the fate has to be seated at its proper place.

Destiny is an ineffably powerful factor, no doubt, but *karma* or action is also not lesser in any way. We don't wish that a conflict takes place between the two, but we would very much like to achieve a state of balance amongst both. If the rhythmic dance of *karma* could be performed dexterously against the backdrop of destiny then it would be an ideal situation, a desired entrance into the realm of happiness.

We think so, or we feel that happenings do occur, with or without reason, or they do not happen at all. From our present point of situation in time and space, we cannot determine whether in future such incidence will take place or not. Obvious as it is, we can only act and act skillfully by utilizing our freedom of action. All the more, according to quantum physics, at sub-atomic level, the incidences happen even without reason. Therefore, we must always have an optimistic view towards life.

Basis of Experience

The pathway of divine knowledge cannot be found only on the basis of experience, although we can describe our experiences, we can also classify them, and accept or reject them. But they can never be extended outside of the limited territory of our life, our past and the present. They are the bounden forces of time and space of our making. All of our experiences normally are either the treasure of the bygone times or wealth of the present. We cannot think about future on their basis, it would be mere imagination.

However, the experience of revelation and divinity is constructed on self-realization. It is the essence of the Self, of the God, and of the Cosmic Intelligence. It cannot be described in words because words start failing the moment we attempt to describe these celestial sensitization and ecstasy or greater awareness. Sometimes, flashes of such heavenly experiences can be felt in the form of intuition, instinct, flair, subliminal psyche, cognizance, flow and sixth sense; and such divinely flow shows us the 'way'.

All the great achievers: adept yogi, intellectual, scientist, philosopher, researcher, devotee, writer, poet, or artist: **experience at some point or the other in their lives, a spark, a glow, an illumination or a current which fills their being with the elixir of knowledge and opens newer path of brilliance**.

The experiences, making us happy or unhappy in our life, germinate at three levels: mind, speech and action. Mind is the womb of all experiences; it is their store house and their guide conductor as well. When we fail in some undertaking, we become a prey of frustration: excited and in turmoil. This experience makes our mind aggressive and violent; any sort of violence could erupt. Consequently, we behave and act on those lines.

Apart from this, we always desire to live in pleasant and comfortable situation, but if any obstacle or hindrance comes in the way of that cozy feeling, we get possessed by anger, suffocation, disappointment and impotence. Then, where remains prudence, *viveka*, serenity? How much success? These cyclones of our mind start manifesting in our language; we lose nobleness. Ultimately, under the influence of such waves of tsunami, we engage ourselves in negativity and derogative actions.

The experience of 'fear' also misleads us away from the pathways of knowledge. Worries, wild desires, uncertainty, unknown, hazy fear! But it is strange that most of the fears are the 'ghosts of fear' – not real. Fear of death, anxiety of society's reaction, nervousness about infamy, restlessness regarding our fading influence, and on. From mind to thoughts; from thoughts to speech; from speech to actions: this is the sequential chain of experiences on which our fears thrive. If we educate and nurture our mind in a righteous manner, all becomes a rhythm, natural flow: karma as well as upheavals, too.

Self Discipline

In order to find the path of divine knowledge, we shall have to understand the interrelationship between 'reason', 'emotion' and 'sensual-pleasure'. If our discriminative intellect does not get hooked up passionately with desires and hunger for redundancy, then the 'reason' and 'logic' may extend their helping hands in the search of the way. What is right, what is wrong – can be decided by the *viveka*; otherwise who will tell you the truth? It is your life, your responsibility, your judgment! No book of wisdom and no high profile guru can considerably make you a knowledgeable person. Think! Whatever you have done so far in life, good or bad, it was performed on the line of directive of your instinct, intuition, natural tendencies and intellect.

If you are able to fill up our mind with harmony and orderliness, your knowledge will never be disarrayed, or distorted. You can easily diagnose the difference between right and wrong. You may, generally, act in a way that is righteous and helpful to all, and, thus, virtues begin to flow from your personality. But harmony, orderliness and discipline of mind can be achieved only by regulated or controlled dispassion, not by dampening attachment, bashing passion and stinking indulgence. While living in the world, doing all what we are doing; and to renounce or be unattached? Difficult! Yes, it is! But not impossible! Leave the rut, the hackneyed path! Adapt to the roads which are unknown to you! Dare to walk on to uncertain realms! Penetrate the mist which engulfs the light of your consciousness, and enter the smoke screen; then a brilliant glow will appear before your eyes. The pathway to Him will shine forth.

You can start your life anew, afresh today and now, but for that you have to attempt deliberately to make a paradigm-shift, slowly, moving yourself away from grooved daily routine, stale thinking, blinkered activities, material goals and cluttering engagements; by abandoning these absurdities, of course in a phased manner; not abruptly, and by giving a new direction towards 'light and freedom' to your thoughts, you can take a new birth today, now! Reincarnate! Alter your consciousness inside-out!

Thus, the inner conflicts and battle of contradictions within may come to an end. Your individuality metamorphoses into a more dynamic, efficient, smart and cool entity. This is the inception of the journey which leads you from darkness to light. You may begin to realize your own ignorance. To know ignorance is the knowledge in itself.

If you can come face to face with what you don't know, you get transformed into a Karma Yogi; an adept in yoga of action; you will no more be worried about the fruits of your work. As you will start living awakened, in the present, the dead load of the past will wither away in a natural way; so also, you will not be derailed by the ghost of uncertainties regarding the future.

Be awake and active during each moment of the present day. Then see the miracle of happiness in life. This is the tried-and-tested doctrine, but we may prove it again if we follow the route, else not. In reality it is effective, result oriented, hence it is a truth.

One thing more; Love is energy, a power, a formidable force. Not hatred. Not jealousy. It is not a vacuum. Express your feelings of love, then, see: how repulsions, guilty conscious and fear vapourize! *Love is the remedy of all absurdities which flourish in our mind. The formation and attributes of love are infinite; its dimensions are extensive*: from a child up to the God, from Nature up to the Self, from creation to annihilation, there pervades a pure, selfless, nonphysical, transcendental love!

The Hard Question

"Keep your senses under discipline! Control your mind! Crush the conflicts of thoughts!"

"Abide by non-violence, truth, detachment, endearment to all!"

All these directives are difficult to follow. We may preach but to control the senses and their master; the mind, appears to be almost improbable, particularly while living amid the corrupt affairs of the world, and struggling to survive while swimming with sharks! Beside this, all sorts of violence, non-truths, attachment, sensuality, etc., and all negative forces are enlivened by our mind. Do whatever you like, thousand strategies to conquer, in one or the other situation while steering out of a weak moment of life, the piercingly twisting energy of frustration and compactly pressed lava of desires may blast open the thin covering-layer of virtuous order and start flowing around. The vows shatter down, the hard-earned purity gets corrupted and the mind becomes boisterous, rough and vehement. It is an uphill task to control the mind, sometimes appearing to be impossibility. Saints and sages meet their fall. May be, the last phase of life is running out, but desire for sensuous indulgence does not die out. Greed, anger, hatred, passion jealousy: none appears to relax and relent to become mild and amenable. It could be nice to talk about theory of all these goodies, but granitic facts of the situation cannot be ignored as such; whatever is… it is!

Apparently, because of this difficulty, in spite of innumerable attempts made through ages by wise people, teachers, religious preachers and self-realized sages to disperse the knowledge of truth, the mentality of the populace remained at the same level, where it was centuries ago. All the more, it is deteriorating, rolling downhill. Nowhere, in any field, there shines any light.

The so-called centres of knowledge have become disgraceful, almost all have been commercialized. No doubt, glamour, glitter, exhibits, and show and clutter of advertising; all are there, but where is that 'truth' which can usher the masses into the blessed path of divine consciousness and thus their suffering could be subdued?

In search of answers to such hard questions, we shall not have to toil anew because, in advance, the ancient geniuses have already propounded the solutions and deposited in the vault of cultural heritage of wisdom.

We shall revisit this theme in the second-half of this chapter. Let us, for the present, ponder upon what *Gitā* has in its treasure to solve this tangle.

Assent of the *Gitā*

To march ahead, to walk forward, to keep safe oneself from tangles, to achieve self evolution of consciousness: what are the directives of the *Gitā* on this? Let us see:

मात्रास्पर्शास्तु कौन्तेय शीतोष्णसुखदुःखदाः ।
आगमापायिनोऽनित्यास्तांस्तितिक्षस्व भारत ।।

(2:14)

The contacts of senses with objects, O son of Kunti, which cause heat and cold, pleasure and pain, have a beginning and an end; they are impermanent; endure them bravely, O descendant of Bharata.

Pleasure and sorrow, or other conflicts (*dwandas*) of similar vein – such as heat-cold, loss-profit, fame-infamy, life-death

,... and on, are merely unstable stimuli or sensations created in the mind by the sense organs; they are born, they survive for some period of time, then die out. None is immutable, infinite. Therefore, by knowing their transient or fleeting nature, one should not get perturbed by them. Let them come, welcome them, try to remain unfurled and unaffected, and let them depart! This is the path of prudence; you need not control or hold up anything. You are not supposed to trample or crush the tremor and ripple arising from the mind; only thing one must do is to *analyze* and perceive their structure, and to 'see' with total awareness.

विहाय कामान्यः सर्वान्पुमांश्चरति निःस्पृहः।
निर्ममो निरहंकारः स शान्तिमधिगच्छति।।

(2:71)

That man attains peace who abandoning all desires, moves about without longings, without the sense of ego and self-esteem.

The root cause of our suffering is our ego. Through its medium, our selfish tendencies are born, and smitten by self aggrandize; we indulge in accumulating redundant luxury and illogical gluttony for our desires. The ego is the source-spring of all longings and allurement; hence if the origin of longings and attachment could be located, there will be no necessity to forcibly check them. On this, the feeling of 'I-ness', 'my-ness' fades out in itself. And thus showers the eternal peace upon us

Obviously, where remains the question of fighting with the mind in continuity?

The questions which were raised in earlier pages, appear to be somewhat pacified by the above statement. Still further, the *Gītā* enlightens us:

Even intelligent people go on doing karma according to their own natural ways.

If a person is motivated by his own inclination of mind, then he takes his thoughts to be right, and acts accordingly.

Love and hate which sprout in the mind for the purpose of sensual satisfaction, are in fact created by the senses themselves.

Therefore, without being influenced by attraction and repulsion, act for controlling the senses because these senses could cause suffering.

Destroy ignorance by true knowledge; erase all doubts about the Self and surrender in yoga by unison with the Almighty.

By keeping the mind balanced, tranquility dawns in life. This is celestial peace which, in the end, ushers you into the realm of Freedom or Moksha.

The person who works with a deep sense of offering at the altar of the highest ideal, does not involve in excessive attachment and does not nourish a feeling of enmity against anybody; thus he is enlightened by the Cosmic Intelligence.

Whatever work we do, it is essential to have basic knowledge of that act; that means, without understanding, if we go on exerting, we may draw a blank.

The meditation: contemplation, *Dhyāna*, analysis and observation of thoughts with serene poise, stands at a much higher level than that of the *Karma*.

To act without worrying about the result of action is the best course in life. Such conviction of renunciation towards fear and greed of reward showers instant peace upon the *Karma yogi.*

Indicating the essence of *Gyāna*, the *Gitā* illumines:

Absence of arrogance and superiority complex; non-violence of mind, words and acts; sincerity, truthfulness and candour; reverence and faith towards Guru; purity and perfectness; stability, Self-control; *Vairāgya* of senses; absence from self-praise; musing upon birth, old age, illness, death, etc., and the pain associated with them; sensible non-attachment with children, spouse, house, wealth, etc; equanimity of mind in pleasant and unpleasant situations, meditating on *Ātman, Parmātman* and the Cosmos: All this is 'Knowledge'. Opposite to this is ignorance.

We are slowly coming at a point from where we may strike the answers to the hard questions raised in earlier pages. If we take the literary meaning of the above facts of wisdom, we may be caught-up in the whirlpool of still harder questions! Is it possible to follow these advices while living in the world, amid the hostile attack of antagonistic setup of the society, largely?

But, wait a moment! The philosophy of *Gitā* can never be impracticable and unrealistic. Hence, we need to dig out the deeper essence from these teachings.

So, howsoever great person you may be, politeness or softness in behaviour is such a virtue that it makes you dear to all, and your ego turns to be a noble asset for you.

Non-violence; not to hurt any creature or Nature, fills your being with the light of divinity. Self-control: while living amongst innumerable problems, to remain unruffled by their effects, is to be taken as *Vairāgya*, renunciation. But to avoid them or to run away from them, yet be mentally attached to them, is not *Vairāgya*; it is hypocrisy.

Whatever sufferings and pains exist in life, they come and shall flow in life incessantly, but to get entangled in them, be depressed, or to narrate them without pause, is foolishness.

'Control your mind;' 'bring your senses under staunch-discipline;' 'annihilate conflicts of thoughts;'... all this means: be aware and alert about problems; awake towards attacks of passion. Smoothen out the wrinkles; nothing will come out of worrying.

Establish your mind in a totally fresh setup. Birth, old age, death: are the natural cycles; go on fighting with problems produced by these stages of life, and be a victor!

Too much of love, inclination, yearning is called 'attachment' (*Āsakti*), which is instigated by desires when our mind comes in contact with worldly things. Have liking, affection, admiration for dear and near ones, objects and events, express your love and tenderness but don't involve in vehemence or restlessness. Look! Let come! Be joyous and then let go! This is the way to control desires.

To keep our wealth and family in close quarters, to secure and maintain them and to be custodian of as well as to be affectionate towards them is not a negative behaviour. It is our duty as well as it is a provider of happiness to others, too. But at the same time, we should not abandon our clear thinking and judgment in such situations. Keeping the 'Wheel of change' in mind, we must maintain calm, a balance, and security of our inner self so that suffering may not enter therein.

Even if an eventuality of dissociation from the things or endeared ones arises, don't disintegrate, crumble down or be devastated. Lament, cry, repent, but then take it in a stride as 'the wish of the All Powerful', and then just get out of the mire. Otherwise, your objective will remain unfulfilled: and the objective is to attain the highest state of mental freedom, eternal peace and divine bliss.

By practising with efforts, one can achieve permanent balance of mind, even if the condition is violently agitating, pleasant or unpleasant!

However, in order to absorb and assimilate the above mentioned merits and excellence, it is mandatory that we learn to concentrate and focus our mind. This is the only technique, the only way. To meditate, cogitate, reflect upon the Creator and the Self with totality of being, may take you to the highway of realization. Thus, if one tries to meet one's destination, the ultimate objective, which is the unison with the Absolute (*Para Brahman*), the Divine Freedom (*Mukti*) could be easily attained.

In the end, Lord Krishna promises:

One who gets liberated from arrogance and delusion, one who conquers the fanciful attachment, one who remains connected with the consciousness, one who can monitor the wildly dancing desires, one who remains unperturbed amidst the raging waves of contradiction of life; reaches up to the pinnacle of the target (i.e., the salvation).

While living and doing actions in the world, if we offer our being unto the Cosmic Energy and the Infinite Intelligence, then by the Grace of that creative power we are bestowed ecstasy: *Parmānanda*. His light and His power become the source of our intellect; such is the Grace of the Almighty. Because of the inflow of such *Viveka* and *Vairāgya,* our individuality brightens up and the enlightenment showers upon our existence; then no tsunami cyclone within the mind can make us unhappy.

We need to repeat Gāyatri mantra for gaining in knowledge, confidence and peace as: "In the Gāyatri mantra (metre) which is the essence of all adoration in Vedas, it has been prayed for: "O Lord! The Creator of the Universe, the root cause of all! We bow unto you; and pray to graciously fill our intellect with the light of consciousness."

It is neither begging for fulfillment of any desire, nor a longing for wealth or power. It's only an aspiration for pure knowledge.

Modern View-point

To search the path of light we need a sharp discriminative awareness, pointed world-wisdom and burning motivation to attain spiritual consciousness. Recognize instantaneously the truth and the non-truth. We are endowed with freedom to act by Nature, therefore we must involve in *karma*; we may escape talking and thinking about the future birth – matters little, but some fruits of the *karma* of the present also ripe in this very birth as well. Obviously, responsibility is ours.

Of course, after performing *karma* in a planned, righteous way, do not afraid of the fate; that is, as far as possible, keep silence about it. We are not capable or powerful even to talk about the future or the destiny. Those who broadcast verbose rhetoric about these spheres of Nature, delude themselves as well as others.

The experiences you have earned so far in life are indeed valuable. The technical, scientific or other practical skills are assets for survival. But always reassess your emotional experiences and sensations of consciousness. Analyze these manifestations of the divine energy in your life.

We may get the answers of 'hard question' only when we ourselves search for them intently. The wisdom of the *Gitā* and that of the wise of the ancient shows us the way regarding the 'hard question':

- Change your path from ignorance to the divine knowledge.
- Live in the present moment; only the present is the reality.
- Dead load of the past and the mist of future will not allow you to progress ahead.
- Truth and love are the reflection of the God.

- Be vigilant about the ego, try to understand its moves, but don't struggle with it.
- Love all but do not get attached.
- Continue to gain prosperity but don't plunge into it.
- When the 'time' batters you, be dejected, grieve and mourn. But don't get shattered into pieces.
- Understand the language of senses and desires but never transform them into frustration.
- Do *karma* yet remain plugged with *Ātman* at all time.
- Don't ask God for anything of your desire; only for the light of consciousness.
- Only the calm, stable, kind and faithful person is granted freedom. Then such a being is not afraid of death.

These are the pathways to the light of consciousness, gateway to freedom, purpose of life, meaning of our birth and four dimensions of *Purusārtha*, fulfillment and ascent of the true religion – the law of the Eternal Light!

•

Symphony – 5

In the world, several streams of knowledge are flowing continuously filled with invaluable transparent grace of energy and peace of devotion. All religions, each centre of philosophy have been advocating, since millennia, the mantras for the art of living, equations of joyous life, pathways of bliss and techniques to fly free in the blue sky. Amongst these, some are complex, some simple while the rest are general or of common rank which, even without the help from an adept, we may learn by common sense.

But for a layman, most of the sermons remain convolutions and reticulations, because he has to struggle hard within the muddle of practicality in the world; he has to confront with granitic truth of life where his logic cannot remain connected with morals or values. In other words, 'survival of the fittest' is a law of nature, i.e., only the best and the strongest will remain alive; the weaklings will extinct. And for living safely and effectively for as long as possible, one must strive, wrestle or exchange blows. How can one follow the rules of love, honesty, non-violence (of any sort) and simplicity?

This argument appears to be correct, and in varied meanings it is true, no doubt! While swimming with sharks, how can one keep the virtues decorated on a platter? In the modern context, where rampant cut-throat contentions dominate the social scenario, where legs are pulled by alligators, and where all the standard criteria of honesty and ethics have been skillfully altered, how can one keep the noble values and feelings of selfless service in safe custody?

Therefore, it is urgent to make pathways to knowledge as simple and intelligible as possible; and it is the need of the time to project the practical applications, in the given circumstances, of the power of yoga, consciousness and devotion to the Lord.

1. How to Achieve the Target?

Too much of practical thinking is generally mechanical; entwined in materialism. Mostly the hard-core practical-minded persons show little inclination towards sentiments, feelings, humane values or high ideals. "If we glue ourselves with illusionary idealism, how can we reach to our goal?" such thoughts appear to be natural for those who choose to walk on the smooth-looking ground of selfishness and fortune-hunting. They go on altering the means in accordance with their goals; this could be understood as; the purpose of their life remains, in any way, to satiate their desires. The targets change, so also the means to attain them and also the desires; then where is stability, *tranquility* and ripple-less serenity?

We have seen in the earlier pages that desires are never satisfied, can never be fulfilled. Obviously, we are caught up in the vicious circle of 'means and aim' yet we always feel empty. Hence we can pacify our wild longings on the basis of wisdom of the *Gitā*; we may understand their *modus operandi*, their nature; subsequently, the method leading to gratification and satisfaction of desires could also be made *Sāttvik,* righteous and empathic.

2. Highway to Divine Life

In the world there are innumerable cultures, civilizations, religions, faiths, cults and beliefs, policies, 'isms', nations and notions, places and regions. So are the ways and means of daily life-style, criteria of good and bad deeds, skilled manners and colours of success, which differentially decide: what is an ideal life and what is not! This diversity ramifies extensively, with nuance of shades in colours and tunes, hence it appears, at times, that the 'ideal life style' of each individual has a different structure; even within one society, in a single category of humans and, all the more, even for every member of a family, a separate measurement, yardstick, standard exists for his/ her idealism!

Then, how can one reach to the highway of ideal life and life divine? What is the recognition mark of a model, an admirable life, because through ages, during the historical times, bearing the upheavals of political turmoil, such concepts of good life had been changing continuously?

How do we believe ideal virtues are benedictory to human beings? Because till yesterday, the behaviour which were classified as 'sins', today the very karma have entered the main stream of our social life. The disrepute of yester years have taken up the garb of nobleness in current years. Nothing remained uncorrupted. Honesty, character, love, clemency, spirituality or reliability has been contaminated in varied degrees. The reason for this landslide is the blending of self interest, sensuality and ego.

Now, a total virtuous life seems to be impossibility. Therefore, in a retreating mode, let us leave ideal life for the present, and talk about a *righteous way of living*: a perfect, balanced and worthy existence. But it is difficult, as well. What shall we do, then? How to walk on the royal road of ultimate joyous life? How to have cognizance of the purpose, meaning, intent, design and destination of our coming to this planet; the Earth? Even if we know the purpose of our birth, as human, then how can we fulfill that mission?

To achieve this purpose, some of the accomplishments are recognized globally: fitness of the body, prosperity earned judiciously, adaptation of divine law of life, fulfillment of desire for comfort and procreation and freedom from pain-giving attachment. Only the love, rhythmic relationships, harmony in the family and personal liberty need to be nourished. However, we may immediately see that these characteristics of a 'worthy life' start entering the periphery of the 'ideal life', but we concluded earlier that the ideal life remains an impossible fantasy.

On reaching to this critical point, or the threshold of a sudden change, we shall have to take the support of the eternal divine Knowledge; then only we may be able to synchronize the notes of *'worthy life'*, *'ideal life'* and *'practical life'*.

Otherwise, a thirst for grasping the highest, a vacuum for piety, and guiltiness of not having a world-wisdom may always chase our psyche.

Hence, let us try the following directives and then walk according to these rules:

All theories, concepts or doctrines in the world are somewhere and somewhat incomplete, illogical and mutable; they change in the flow of time and space. Therefore, even if you are unable to follow them in entirety, don't become a prey of inferiority complex.

If we look at things with a wider perspective, we will find 'good' or 'bad' is a relative expression – not an absolute characteristic.

We look for the evaluation of our deeds by other people; we are always anxious about the opinions of other person about our individuality; thus we lose our freedom.

We should not always try to meet the expectation of all and sundry. We can never fulfill the hopes and desires of others.

As far as possible, keeping your existence safe and secured, adopt the path of honesty, cooperation, succor and support to the destitute, propriety in karma, some contribution towards humanity, non-violence of all kinds, practice of sympathetic behaviour towards the needy, and justifiable earning of the wealth.

On one hand, our undisciplined desires dance wildly and on the other, the pull of the rules of morality of all sorts, acts upon us. The two factors go on struggling within; day-in-and-day-out; in view of this fact, however, we cannot live a worthy and just life unless we follow the principles laid down by ancient sages: this leads us to the *Abhyāsa* of *Dhyāna*, *Dān* (giving), *Tapa*, study of scripture, company of wise persons, total surrender to the Almighty and the absence of the killing passion.

Almost all of us make our plan to earn wealth, follow the law of living, procure, means for happiness by meeting the desires and to attain the freedom from all at the end of the show. However, these aims should be made simple, easy, logical, humane, soft, balanced and contented so that in the life-long process of attaining the targets, we may not have to depend upon deception and falsehood, fraud, bluff and juggling, violence, or other unethical methods.

Against the backdrop of overall knowledge, we must always try to understand our present position, i.e., where are we standing today? While taking decision about worldly affairs, one has to scrutinize the desires as well as the values of life.

Every person holds upon his own firm convictions, his commitments and basic elements of the existence. While solving the tangles of life, one must keep an eye upon one's convictions about values of life.

Never abandon your solid ground of goodness, may be you were to do some reconditioning to match the time and space of your positioning.

Every person has an individualistic style of working. We also have one specific way to meet the challenges. Therefore neither one should criticize nor compare oneself with others. Of course, keeping your faith intact and managing your survival skillfully, act according to the circumstances, which is known as *Yugadharma*.

Suppose you are caught up in some contradictory situation, from where your exit appears difficult, then, cleverly protect your purpose and your conviction. Even then, if the situation does not come under control, change a bit of your aim and also the angle of your values. Let the events happen, face them boldly and then let them go. Never lose the joyous state of mind and peace of the self!

We have to continue walking on the path of life by keeping the hard reality of the world in mind; then we have to pay full attention to righteousness of approach and to try for ideal means. We have to constitute our doctrine, our principles, our equations of rules and regulations and our faith, belief and yard stick for real happiness.

Life is ours: We must search the way ourselves!

3. It is the Game of Balance

The two main aspects of immanence in the teaching of the *Gitā* are: First: to keep equipoise in all circumstances, and the second: while doing karma, to offer all to the Almighty. Under the extended definition of these two aspects, all expressions of self-realization could be classified and subsequently they could be imbibed as simplified directives in modern context:

The field of equanimity of mind contains absolute peace: equilibrium, calmness, temperance, patience and steadiness of *Viveka.* All these words (and the ideas they carry) are applied to a balanced life. Comfort or discomfort at the body level, fame or infamy at the mental level, life or death at emotional level: these situations are symbolic. Related to these modalities there exist several positive and negative spheres which in continuity make us happy or unhappy.

By making intentional efforts, practice, and by pondering, we may escape the high and low tides of these forces. Then think:

- All is mutable, unstable and momentary.
- No one will remember you through the flow of the gushing time.

- *Tapa* (penance) develops the power of endurance.
- Nothing is more valuable treasure than the serenity of mind.
- Suffering of our mind could be subdued by helping the deprived and destitute.
- Our ego becomes friendly if we attempt to make our mind quiet.
- If the mind does not vibrate, my world cannot make me restless.
- The *Samsār* (world in its totality) of sufferings is nothing but a creation of my mind which changes colours on the screen of past experiences.
- The mind can be stabilized by *Dhyānyoga* or other techniques of concentration.

The laws of Nature do not operate according to our desires or needs, neither they are dependent upon our emotions and our reactions towards pain or pleasure. In the same way, the rules of logic, mathematics or physics do not require to take permission from anybody for functioning. All these operate according to the intellect of Nature, Cosmic Mind or the plan of the Absolute Energy. We know as well as we do not know these laws, rules and patterns.

'Do your work, but surrender all to that power'; means, we have liberty to act; we are not merely bonded by destiny, but still many things happen which we cannot predict: unknowable in advance. In that situation we find ourselves helpless and incapable of doing anything. Hence, *Karmayoga* (the yoga of action) is the best doctrine – "do your *karma*, don't leave anything on fate; pick up courage to take responsibility and then leave the steering wheel of the outcome of your *karma* in His hands". By this principle, one gets the answers of all the questions regarding fate, freedom and catastrophe. This is a useful, a practical philosophy; that is why it has been designated by the wise as 'the best'.

Bond of Union with *Ātman*

In connection with the divine knowledge, it has always been narrated – 'Know yourself'. Get attached to your *Ātman*. The ego is that part of the spirit which remains veiled by ignorance, but as soon as the blanket of mist is removed, the light of the Self shines forth'. And so on. What is the meaning of all this? Generally we do not know the *Ātman*; then how to get plugged with that phenomenon?

We are well aware of this fact that inside our physical body there lives a dynamic centre, or a point (that is connected to each part i.e. it pervades all), which keeps our life throbbing, makes the sense organs activated and supplies uninterrupted electric current into the brain. At the background of all organs, nervous system, circulatory system, pulsating heart and sparking neurons of the brain, there exists a 'living thing' which incessantly fills the energy fuel in them. Our thoughts, feelings, emotions, instincts, intuitions and experience of pain and pleasure – all are born from the womb of some energy, command, or sovereignty; but alas, as soon as that power withdraws, its manifestation, our body, turns into a corpse. This energy is *Prāna,* but there has to be a master of this *Prāna*! He is without attributes, but He is Almighty; He is invisible, but when expression of Grace is revealed, He appears to be a spectacle vista. He is our existence in totality. He is our *Ātma-tatva* (the essential spirit) about which innumerable treatises have been written through millennia and definitions; formal and concise statements about meaning; have been prescribed.

Here, at this juncture, we have to perceive that the Self is our existence, our entirety, our completion, our core individuality – in the cosmic context.

To get connected with the *Ātman* means to unveil our own existence in all aspects of its nature, to conceive its essence, to *analyze*, to get a glimpse, and to enter relationship of such Cosmic being with other dimensions of Nature.

First of all, we must know the affiliation of our desires with our mind and ego. 'I want to have this; someone possesses this; I do not have that; if I get this, I will become happy'. Fabulous wealth, ever-newer taste, attractive beauty, exciting music, unparallel luxury, heavenly- indulgence, feline touch, intoxicating perfumes, and so on. These so-called pleasure-giving devices appear to be happiness-giver, to certain extent, but ultimately they are pain-generative because they do not remain forever and our physical and mental capacity to 'enjoy' them also goes on depleting.

Then, does it mean, we dump away all our pleasures and comforts? Shall we become a rock or a feeling-less dried and dead wood?

This is not a solution of the problem. We can neither control our mind nor crush our desires. Beside this, the action of our senses is necessary for our fitness, security and calmness in life. If we turn the meter of all senses to a 'zero', and put the mind under heavy clutches, our remaining alive may become impossibility.

Then what to do? The answer to this tangle has been already provided by saints and sages of the olden times, which is narrated in the wisdom books of the ancient. 'Self-control, Self-discipline'. But be aware! This self-control does not mean what has been erroneously taught to us. No self-control can be attained by forcible tactics, by application of raw strength, adamancy, or torturous methodology. We may reinterpret 'Self-discipline' in a newer way that our relationship with our desires and longings should he comfortable, loose, detached, lax, indifferent, or like a stranger. Not as horse-riding.

The desires must not overcast our mind. They should not be naggers. A madness for sensual indulgence becomes disastrous to our peace of mind. The relationship with the desires should be somewhat neutral, indifferent, or stranger-like. As soon as a desire arises, try to understand the degree of happiness it may produce, if fulfilled, and also look for the result of the whole game. Then one may attend to it in a righteous manner – or let it go! Because beyond this also, our existence will continue to thrive, our Self will radiate; we need no such excitement of short-lived pleasure.

If we are able to make out and to do assessment of our shortcomings, emptiness, lacking and imperfections, we smoothly arrive at the road to revelation. Suppose we are filled up to the eye-brow with bitterness, hatred, jealousy, arrogance, lust, greed, etc., and we do not have any idea about this sludge, we may take for granted that we are sage and wise being; then we may easily visualize the result of all this. Nobody will openly tell us about our demerits and vice. We have to weed them out by picking up tactfully and by winnowing. Beyond this stage, we may not require any attempt to stamp on the desires; they will become peaceful and logical in themselves.

The core essence of unison with *Ātman* relates to: develop a cognizance of your entire individuality; observe the mind and your longings; treat them as if they are dubious strangers because they do not arise from the deeper levels of your existence.

Don't believe them without probing, otherwise they may cheat you!

But it must not be concluded from these talks that you just become a doll of clay, or a door-mat! Don't leave your dynamic nature, don't evade actions; keep managing your prosperity and security; live a full-sized life! Smile! Even enjoy hearty laughter; sunshine of the mind! But in any case, don't get entangled into the net of chameleonic desires!

Let us ponder upon some more points in this regard:

- During meditation *analyze* the desires.
- Give a new direction to your existence.
- Identify those factors which instigate your senses.
- Meet your longings as if they are strangers!
- Keep a relationship of indifference with the forces of the mind.
- Look at your subsistence with a new angle.
- Change the path; walk on uncertain and unknown route.
- Find out the causal factors of sufferings.
- Abandon this conviction that you are an enlightened and accomplished person.

Keeping the self-discipline as a base, let pain and pleasure come and without being devastated let them go! If your pleasure and joy diminish, even then don't get tortured and miserable.

Practice of *Viveka* and continual association with wisdom, can keep you connected with Supreme Being and your Self.

•

Resonance – 5

The world is an 'illusion' or the 'truth'?
This mirage is perceived to none,

Clean ken and wash the thoughts!
Then only one can know: all are only 'One'.

One may listen, sermons by priests,
Or may read treatises by the sages wise,
But, first of all scan them all,
Search for 'reason' with eagle's eyes.

Mind is the product of physical brain,
World is the painting of impression's light,
Here dances the cyclonic whirl,
Pain or pleasure, wrong or right!

If the desires can't be controlled,
With folded hands then bow them best!
'Hai', 'Hallow! With plastic smile,
Treat it as an unwanted guest.

Look at the world as glittering show,
Or, a dance of drunken wild;
It's a chance that we are here, and
Facing days and nights, harsh or mild.

Don't sink deep in worldliness,
Stand away, and a bit absent,
Weave stronger insight and psyche,
Live in the 'Now', the passing present

Your *Ātman* is the Self and Light,
Spread the light: throughout the space,
Dissolve the beginning, merge the end,
Truth of Being, it's the Grace.

Balance is the name of the game,
In mind and heart: at ease and quiet,
Offer the fruits of karma to Him
Spread the wings and touch the height.

Think! When there is darkness, dense
Then only the light will flow,
Weed-out the thorns of lust and vice,
Stride in knowledge, steady and slow.

Life is a soft, rhythmic song,
Mellifluous, smooth and even,
If we follow Nature's tune
All will be happy and home: the heaven!

•

Take in a Stride – 5

After you have studied and listened all, search the path of truth by yourself.

Don't trample the desires; keep only a disjunctive, polite relation with them.

It is not necessary that all incidences happen because of an obvious cause.

Fully utilize your liberty of action in a justified manner.

Then take the responsibility of your *karma*, too.

Our life is very simple, easy and graceful; live your life fully and squarely.

Shake hand with happiness, and then let go.

Embrace grief, and then let go.

The aims of your life must be reasonable and just.

The means to achieve these aims have to be more righteous.

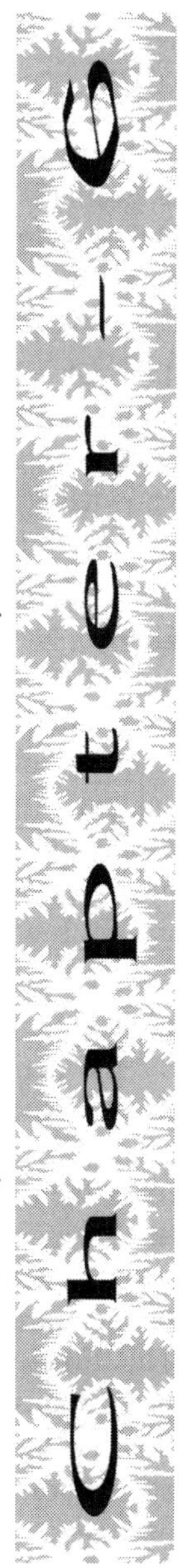

Infinite Energy of the Cosmos

The human intelligence is not capable of accurately assessing the totality of cosmic energy; our mind is captive of time-space; it is limited while the Creative Power is free from these bondages. All the dimensions, too, are the creation of that Force. We can draw only some raw inference and make few limited scientific observations to estimate fraction of that Infinite Almighty, that omnipotent which gave birth to the universe, which produced all galaxies, their planets, astronomical bodies, the sun, the moon, the earth, and so on. Every iota of the cosmos is governed by well-defined laws; all the celestial bodies are balanced by gravitational force, moving since billions of years in their own orbits without deviation; even the changes and deviations are fixed and follow a definite pattern; yet the whole system does not collapse, fail or come to a naught!

Beside this outer wonder, see the smaller entities! The creatures of our planet earth, floras and faunas and the man! Then, the highest mental faculties, mind, intellect, discriminative skill and the phenomenal Self, all functioning within the existential gamut of the man, trying consistently to perceive the infinite energy as well as the Creator. Strange! All wonderful: natural laws, electromagnetic, gravitational, geomagnetic and atomic power, and life, death and consciousness in living beings.

Science has contributed commendably in this direction, although while walking on this path science had to battle with religious fanaticism, illogical beliefs and stale theories; and to certain extent, such thorns even today prick the reason-based knowledge: fanaticism and blinkered beliefs clash in continuum with analytical study of natural phenomena!

The foundation of the modern science was laid down by Galileo, Newton, Maxwell, and Darwin during sixteenth through nineteenth centuries. In addition, thousands of devoted scientists have contributed invaluably by their hard work, to varied branches of knowledge. During the first-half of the twentieth century, Albert Einstein has changed the model of physics and cosmology, thitherto accepted for a long time. We shall now have a glimpse of 'creation' against the background of scenario which is widely established till today:

About 12 billion years ago, a mega-event happened in the void which is named as 'Big-Bang' ('*sphota'* called by Indians) by the astrophysicists. Why it occurred? How it occurred? Explicit and clear-cut answers to these questions are not known to us, but still it has been indicated and testified on the basis of mathematical equations as well as astrophysical derivations that in some region of the extensive space, the quanta of energy fused together; this was possible because of the extremely high temperature which subsequently resulted into a colossal bang. The 'time' was born at this point. The temperature of the Bing-Bang locus was about one hundred billion degree Kelvin in the first hundredth part of the first second (of time); and also at that point, the density was 3.8 billion times higher than that of water.

In the beginning, there were only 'quarks' present in the region which are infinitesimal ultra-micro entities, even finer than the particles of an atom. These quarks when condensed produced other micro-entities, such as: hadrons, proton, neutron, lepton (electron, neutron), etc. These are specialized terminologies, no doubt, but this can be perceived distinctly that in the beginning there were no atoms; the atoms were evolved after the Bing-Bang when the basic unit of energy; the quarks, were condensed into the 'bigger' units.

After this event, by mixing up of the helium and lithium gases, hydrogen was produced. As the region of the Big-Bang started cooling, at about three thousand degree Kelvin temperature, the electrons and the nuclear structure united with each other and a stable atom was born.

Thereafter, the particles of light – named as 'photons' (which are 'particles' as well as energy waves) extended enormously and cooled down to 3 degree Kelvin temperature; by the process of radiation these photons spread out through the universe. Subsequently, the atom cooled down, condensed, and gave rise to various astronomical bodies.

• The rest of the story is generally known and the origin and evolution of life on the earth have been mostly ascertained by scientific studies.

And, the man is decorated with the crown of excellence in the drama; so far!

According to Mundakapanishada:

"That is *Akshar Brahman*, the Truth. As from immense fire, innumerable sparks are emitted out continuously, O' *Soumya*, in the same manner, from that *Akshar Brahman* several subsistence and manifestations appear forth and then get absorbed in the same.

From this *Akshar Purush* originates 'breathing' (life) and also from the same the mind, all senses, space, air, radiant energy, water and the earth arise."

Archetype of the Creator

In every religion of the world, the Creator has been described in varied form; every description is a unique inspiration, or one's 'mind's eye'. Also, every faith has structured different process through which the creation has supposedly taken place. The man has made his own image as the basis and then painted the modality of the God, reinforcing such portrayals with reverence, faith and devotion, and then putting it on granitic foundation.

The fundamentals of the religions are mostly metaphysical, subjective concepts while those of the scientific analysis rest on the objective observations and experimentations. In any case, we cannot dump any one of them as such, yet we may redefine and reinterpret, with wider perspective, the concept of religious teachings; keeping scientific parameters in view. To exemplify this approach, we may cite the cases of atomic physics where it has been proved beyond doubt that the particles emitted by the atoms become energy waves and, at times, the energy waves convert themselves into the particles; all the more, this swapping, or inter-change, could be controlled by the thoughts of the scientist; the experimenter, so as to which form, energy waves or particles, he wishes to see! This phenomenon is directly related to our concept that whether God is with a form *Sākār*; the particle, or He is without a form *Nirākār*; the energy wave. Both situations are true and they depend on your belief or your way of wishing to look at them.

We normally visualize *Ishwara* in configuration of living being, including humans, but if we could think that the Almighty is the nucleus of inexhaustible energy, we may be able to bring religion and science in adjacency. In the same way, we can define the time-scale in the magnitude of cosmic measurement instead of time-measuring parameters designed by man; the Cosmic Time is much extensive than our 'time'. Also, we can interpret that various gods and goddesses represent centres of power that are active at various levels of time and space as a part of regulatory system of the universe.

It all means that we should take science as a lighthouse to decipher the real meaning of stories and parables of ancient writings, under the light of reason, cause and effect. This is not disbelief or atheism, rather it is to strengthen the wisdom of the past by fresh newness and regency. Don't go after word-to-word meanings of our scripture or the books of wisdom; try to unveil the deeper essence, and redefine it!

Scientifically the theory of Big-Bang is almost well-established today. Thereupon, it has been postulated that by the force of primordial energy, the universe is expanding in continuum and the velocity of its expansion is more than that of light! Therefore, we can't know the boundary of our universe; neither we can see it nor derive it mathematically because our techniques of measurement can't surpass the speed of light.

Yet it sounds logical that when the force of the Big-Bang will slow down in the far future, the universe shall start contracting or shrinking, and in the end of the process of collapsing, the totality of the universe will revert to an infinitesimal 'dot' to get absorbed in its own cause of energy source. The scientists have named it as Big-Crunch: Big-Bang...Big-Crunch! The Upanishads have already narrated these phenomena millennia back as *Shrishti* and *Pralaya* or *Srijan* and *Vilaya*.

The Stream of Never-ending Flow

Ordinarily, the universe appears to us as a stationary and inert system but it is not so; it is a throbbing and pulsating organism. It is an uninterrupted stream, a flow, a cosmic continuum. At periphery the cosmos is spreading, expanding; at places within, some regions is undergoing a process of condensation; at others, newer bodies are being created or the existing ones getting annihilated. But, mind it: all happens within the frame-work of physical laws of Nature: nothing occurs erratically. All creation, each and every plan and design, functions because of the power-packed energy behind it. It is strange that in such a system of infinite extent, nothing new is created and nothing is lost from the sum total of energy or the matter! All remains constant!

Beginning from the origin of a single-celled creature up to the advent of man, the whole story relates the process of evolution. (Why did the process of evolution of other genres, living beings stopped after the evolution of man?) The forces of Nature which push the organic evolution towards the destiny are:

Struggle for existence

Natural selection

Survival of the fittest

Continued progressive pressure of energy

The whole scheme of the cosmos is complex but intelligent, as it is in a flawless operation since billions of years, that too in a progressive mode. It is strange that all is dynamic, all appears to be complicated yet all is based upon simple and easy laws.

Scientifically speaking, about 4.5 billion years ago, the one-celled life originated; their structure was simple. Those organisms (plants or animals) were the ancestors of bacteria. In the vast spread of time through which the ever busy evolution continued, the DNA and gene-bearing chromosomes evolved in these pre-bacterial organisms. The nature continued to bestow life with the faculty of memory. The forces of mutation in genetic material, the change in environment and struggle for existence amongst the species made the organisms to evolve continuously. At every level of time, there were innumerable chances or probabilities; within the circumscription of physical, chemical and biological laws, the animate beings which could survive on the basis of their best fitness, extended their progeny: the off springs which were capable of living competently and reproducing further. This was a journey from simplicity to more efficient complexity.

About 20 million years ago, the ape species was evolved in which the Gibbon, Siamong, Orangutan, Gorilla, Chimpanzee, Booboos and 'Homo family' group have appeared on the scene; they came as branching of the ape family, originated from a single group but ramified into a branched system. Thereafter, ape-man was evolved from the stock of 'Homo' group. About 5-6 million years ago, the pre-man family came into existence, which exhibited characteristics of man as well as ape. And in the end, at about 60 thousand years ago, the modern man came on the stage. The man has liberty to act. No other species of animals enjoy this freedom.

On the basis of scientific studies, it has been postulated that the cosmos quivers and vibrates within the spheres of probabilities, but every incidence is not born of destiny. Energy of Action (*karma*) is also a main factor; then natural laws and unknown plans and pathways of the centres of cosmic forces also control the melodrama.

You may ask –"how does all this connects with Tsunami of our mind? How can the story of evolution; may it be a hard-core scientific structure; reduce my sufferings and pains? How can all these talks help the millions of helpless masses in this world?"

The question is justified and difficult, too; however these accounts, take us from ignorance towards knowledge; of course, in the context of insight into the physical world.

The science answers to the blind faith so that the limitation of your mind's eye could be removed. This is not atheism, disbelief; rather this is a solid ground of faith. If several of your troublesome questions are answered, and some of your tangles regarding the creation, infinite energy, our own origin, and free rein of probabilities given by Nature are straightened out by the above brief description, then this story could be meaningful in diminishing your tension and sufferance.

However, several problems which generate unhappiness arise also from social, financial, political, geographical, religious, cultural and historical phenomena. A search for their solution could be made by thoroughly changing the attitude towards life; with *Viveka* and *Vairāgya*.

Lastly, in spite of very odd situation, our reaction and behaviour towards worldly happenings are the causal factors of our happiness or unhappiness. The happenings or events do not contain any pain or pleasure in them; it is generated through our philosophy towards each event. What decides whether our personal life is a heaven or a hell? : Our prudence, knowledge of spirituality, dexterity to face the challenges and capability to adapt to the flow of life.

Now, we shall see, what has been expounded by the *Gitā* about origin, existence and absorption of the universe. This wisdom should be interpreted by way of simile, metaphor, allegory, analogy; not in the form of word-to-word meaning. Beside this, the man-made parameters of time, distance, concept of space and all other mental, intellectual, physical experiences as well as dimensions are different from that of the universal system. God's logic is not our logic and His reasons are not our reasons. Then, how can we know the unknowable? Our scales of measurement are minuscule, limited and mostly uncertain. His scales are unlimited yet certain. Obviously, only by keeping an open mind and a wide-angled view, we may be able to realize the wisdom as declared by Sri Krishna.

The Creation of the World According to the *Gitā*

Before the 'creation' it was an infinite void (*Mahā Shoonya*). Only the *Brahman* was there: Infinite, Beginning-less, Endless, Omnipotent, *Para Brahman*. Only by a thought wave of the *Brahman*, Nature originated which is the formation of Cosmic Illusion (*Mahā Māyā*). From *Prakriti* and *Purush*, or *Māyā* and *Brahman*, (Nature and Spirit), originated the Cosmos (*Brahmānd*); so is the verdict of *Upanishad*.

The *Gitā* has illuminated the essence of this knowledge. We shall dwell upon few selected pointers on this aspect:

भूमिरापोऽनलो वायुः खं मनोबुद्धिरेव च।
अहंकार इतीयं मे भिन्ना प्रकृतिरष्टधा।।

(7:4)

Earth, water, fire, air and ether, mind, intellect, egoism: these are My eightfold ***Prakriti****. This is mine* ***Aparā Prakriti*** *(inert Nature).*

अपरेयमितस्त्वन्यां प्रकृतिं विद्धि मे पराम्।
जीवभूतां महाबाहो ययेदं धार्यते जगत्।।

(7:5)

This is the lower Prakriti; different from it, O Mighty-armed, know My higher ***Prakriti****, the very life-element by which this world is upheld.*

Sri Krishna had meticulously explained the twin concept of matter (Nature) and energy (Spirit, *Ātman*): The inert Nature is the matter, and the live Nature is energy. The former is lowly placed; the latter is higher in position. Because of the presence of *Jeeva* (spark of *Purush, Ātman*), the inert matter (or lower Nature) remains live, pulsating and throbbing.

Both dimensions are different: body, mind, intellect, ego is extrinsic or alien and perishable; but the *Ātman* is intrinsic and immortal. Unfortunately, we connect our *Ātman* with our body; we take it for sure that our Self, or *Ātman*, is same as our body, mind, intellect and ego; hence we suffer the pang of misplacement or miss identity.

But when the Self is identified as a centre of light, separated from the inert body and mind, etc., then all our sorrows come to an end. And the Eternal Bliss dawns upon our life!

The Self (*Ātman*) is *Brahman*. This is the subsistence, *terra firma* of the whole universe. Our own world is the formation of several dimensions: physical stretch outside and emotional expansion within! But the source fountain of the whole cosmos originates from mere thought wave in the Mind of the Creator.

These two *Prakritis* are the womb of all beings. So I am the source and dissolution of the whole universe.

It is also expounded that –

*Infinite Self (**Ātman**) is the Truth, the rest is imposed upon Him, hence one, who recognizes **Ātman**, knows one's own real 'nature'. **Karma** is a subtle energy which is generated by creative instinct and remains in the backdrop of every action.*

Regarding the definition of 'Time', it has been narrated that by applying the parameters of human standards, the cosmic Time cannot be measured. Within the sphere of such divine time the occurrence of 'birth' and 'demise' of the universe goes on incessantly.

सहस्त्रयुगपर्यन्तमहर्यद्ब्रह्मणो विदुः।
रात्रिं युगसहस्त्रान्तां तेऽहोरात्रविदो जनाः।।

(8:17)

Those people who know the length of the day of Brahma which ends in a thousand aeons, and the night which also ends in a thousand aeons, they know day-and-night, i.e., the Time.

We may perceive these relative extents of time in view of the Theory of the Relativity as established by Einstein. All is relative to other phenomenon; nothing is absolute except the One.

Some wise persons have calculated the duration of such divine Eras; they say that one day of *Brahma* (the power-in-charge of creative force) is equal to four billion and three hundred twenty million years of the human's time. Clear as it is, we can very well visualize the tininess of our life's span! Then, why to waste our time in anxiety, hatred, jealousy, violence, sensuous passion and greed of no consequence? Be happy, face the bad weather, and do *karmas* which are positive, intellectually motivating and virtuous!

It has been further said about the creation of the world:

At the dawn of Brahma's day all manifested elements are originated from the un-manifested. At the coming of the night they dissolve verily in that alone which is called Un-manifest. (8:18).

This wheel of heavenly day and night goes on revolving without stopping and the being rotates perpetually through birth-death circle of destiny. But the one who is a *Gyāni* (a wise person knowledgeable about the Absolute) gets liberated from the bondage of the wheel, and verily gets enlightenment. Then such person can never be tortured by the *Klesha* (sufferings and sorrows) of the *Samsār* (*Māyā*).

The path of knowledge is the 'path of light'; the path of ignorance is the 'path of darkness'.

शुक्लकृष्णे गती ह्येते जगतः शाश्वते मते।
एकया यात्यनावृत्तिमन्ययावर्तते पुनः।।

(8:26)

The path of light and the path of darkness available for the world are verily thought to be forever; by the one, the path of light a man goes returns not, by the other, the path of darkness, he returns again.

Perplexity, imbalance, vacillation and uncertainty: create a situation equated to sorrows and sufferings of birth and death and the 'wheel of time'.

All incidences, which give rise to happiness or unhappiness; the killing turmoil in the mind, and all things which appear to be bolt-from-the-blue, take place through the medium of God's Nature (Divine *Prakriti*). By these, our ego experiences pleasure or pain. Obviously, if we could perceive this basic cause-and-effect system, the stings of our disquiet and dejection may become less intensive.

मयाध्यक्षेण प्रकृतिः सूयते सचराचरम्।
हेतुनानेन कौन्तेय जगद्विपरिवर्तते।।

(9:10)

O' Kaunteya, by My power as a Supervisor, the Prakriti (Nature) produces the moving and the non-moving, and because of this the wheel of the universe is revolving.

Whatever happens in the world, it is the reflection of That *Brahman*; therefore, accept that the hard time is also sent by Him, yet try to develop courage to endure it and to solve the problems effectively.

तपाम्यहमहं वर्षं निगृह्णाम्युत्सृजामि च।
अमृतं चैव मृत्युश्च सदसच्चाहमर्जुन।।

(9:19)

As Sun I give heat; I withhold and send the rain; I am immortality and also the death, both existence and non-existence, O Arjuna!

All are equal in the eyes of the God; neither any being is favourite, nor unfavourite to Him. But the one who surrenders unto Him with love, becomes dearest to That One.

In order to explain explicitly, the structure of our mind and also various components of the outer world, it is further declared:

The intellect, ego and five senses of knowing, these seven are the epicentres of energy and receive their power from the Supreme; they are the instruments of Cosmic Mind. The one who recognizes My multi-dimensional radiance and adopts My Mahāyoga, the sufferings of such sage vanish away.

When we dissolve our ego in the Self (*Ātman*) and thereafter remain established in that state of bliss, then by doing so, we invoke the Divine Power: to call upon such a power whose abode is in our heart. By meditating upon our own power of the Self (*Ātma-shakti*), which in Him is the source of infinite energy, the virtuous intellect as well as the knowledge of the *Brahman* dawns upon our being.

Narrating the enormity of power, immensity of grandeur and radiance of beatitude of the *Brahman*, Lord Sri Krishna says that whichever entity is *the best* amongst all formations, that entity represents the Grace of the Almighty *Brahman*. He is the death which annihilates all and He is the cause of the origin of all which takes birth.

In this world, all things and beings can be classified as of the best, the middle and the low states; amongst these three categories, none exists without that cosmic energy; it means, all possess the radiance of that power. This perception helps us to realize His omnipresence and it is also for cognizance of

His *Lilā* (*Mahā Māyā*) at the time of disaster and adversity. All happens within the multi-circled spheres of Nature, under the action of physical laws.

After beholding the Cosmic Form of the God, Arjuna is flabbergasted with bewilderment. He discerns that every component, being or matter, is born from only one source, exists in that, and absorbed back by the same. The death equalizes every one; nothing can escape that pull. If we clearly conceptualize this immutable Truth, we may comprehend the tsunami tornados of our mind and then we can boldly face the consequence.

तथा प्रदीप्तं ज्वलनं पतंगा
विशन्ति नाशाय समृद्धवेगाः।
तथैव नाशाय विशन्ति लोका :
तवापि वक्त्राणि समृद्धवेगाः।।

(11:29)

As the moths rush hurriedly into a blazing fire for their own destruction, so also these creatures hastily rush into your mouths for destruction.

But, still the questions arise – how to survive this terrible situation? How can we attain infinite peace? Where can one find realms of happiness? How can the suffering be eradicated?"

It can be achieved by way of self-discipline, by doing karma without neck-breaking attachment, by not being indulged in enmity, jealously, and hatred, by being in unison with our *Ātman* and by helping the helpless.

मत्कर्मकृन्मत्परमो मद्भक्त संगवर्जितः।
निर्वैरः सर्वभूतेषु यः स मामेति पाण्डव।।

(11:55)

He who does actions for Me, who surrenders to Me, who is devoted to Me, who is free from attachment, and who bears enmity towards none, he comes to Me, O Pāndava!

If we submit our existence to the radiance of the universe and if we live our life with love, piety and dispassion, the pain and upheavals can be laid to rest.

Other Gems to Ponder

- The fragrance of the soil, the brilliance of the fire, the life factor of the living beings and self-sacrifice of the sages: all these are the glimpses of that infinite energy.
- He is the seed of total existence, wisdom of the wise, and beauty of gracious Nature.
- If we contemplate on the Supreme Power, the mist of Great Illusion vanishes away.
- The beings entwined in love and hate, or desire and aversion, and in a long series of conflicting duos, always live in delusion.
- *Brahman* is infinite; His image or reflection is the spiritual revelation, and His creative power, by which the universe originates, is the karma.
- By meditating with the concentrated mind, upon that Highest Abode of the Might, all agonies of life are annihilated, and the Absolute Bliss is attained.
- The path of divine knowledge is a way to serenity; and that of ignorance leads to turmoil.
- Senseless expectations, useless acts, absurd data and information, and stupid thoughts give rise to demoniac nature and behaviour.
- The one, who always reflects upon the grace of the Absolute and the eternal awareness, attains liberty; *Moksha.*

- By training our mind to practise, we may achieve stability and balance in life.
- One who is contented in every situation, steadfast in meditation, self-disciplined, with surrendered mind and intellect, and having un-flickering faith, accomplishes his Highest Goal.

•

Symphony – 6

In context to the physical aspects of infinite cosmic energy, science has now realized certain truth that: 'Energy can never be destroyed; the universe originated after the big-bang; fusion of particles gave rise to atom, then the inert entities and the world of living beings were evolved. The whole universe functions on the basis of physical laws and it will continue to do so infinitely, etc.

But, science does not know as yet: what was before the Big- Bang? From where is the power to carry on the show flowing incessantly? All appears complex, but why it is simple? How were the natural laws formulated and how many more are there which we do not know as yet, although they are working in the world? Before the discovery of 'law of gravity' and 'laws of motion' by Newton, these laws were operative although no one knew about them. This fact can be applied to all scientific knowledge.

Infinite energy, or power, had always been there and so also it shall remain for all time to come; of course, in one or the other form! It remains constant, neither more nor less. It is possible that there are certain laws controlling the material world but the man does not know them – and could be, they might be discovered after several years. Today we are ignorant about them and some incidences could be occurring because of these unknown laws; and we call them miracles! Now, imagine the extent of our own ignorance!

Stephen Hawking mentions:

"Even if we do discover a complete unified theory, still we will not be able to predict events in general. The reason for this is that the uncertainty principle of quantum mechanics sets on our power of prediction. There is nothing we can do to get around that. Beside this, the laws of physics work only in very simple situations, not in the most extreme conditions. We know the basic laws that underlie all of chemistry and biology, yet we have little success in predicting human behaviour from mathematical equations."

What does *Vedānta* Opine?

Since millennia, the opinions of various religions and philosophies regarding the cause and existence of the world are in currency. *Upnishads* have meditated deeply as well as extensively on this subject. *Shwetāshwar Upanishad* narrates that the *Rishis*, the *Brahman Gyānis* (the knower of the subject) raised the questions: "What are the characteristics of the *Brahman*; the root cause of the universe? From what we are formed? By whom, or by whose power we are alive? Who keeps us pulsating? Who gives us impulses, or inspires us to walk on in pain and pleasure during the journey of the *Samsār*?"

After deep thinking on these questions, it was concluded that the time, tendency, or living beings and other such factors cannot be designated as the cause of the world because they get affected by pain and pleasure, or they are conditioned by the *karma*.

In this way, after an intensive analysis of several aspects of this subject, the *Shruti* (*Vedānta*: Essence of Vedas) has declared:

The wise sages who had realization of *Brahman* could discern that no method is capable of perceiving *Brahman*; then *by intensive practice of Dhyāna Yoga, they themselves experienced that Root Cause.*

They had a cognizance - "The *Brahman* is neither a 'cause' (*kārana*) nor a 'non-cause', (*Akārana*), nor different from these two as well. Think of *Māyā* or *Prakriti* (Nature) and of *Māyāvi* (the one who creates illusion) as *Maheshwara* (*Grandeur* of God)".

Sri Krishna says in the *Gitā*, "*With my power, Nature creates living and non-living entities*".

The disciple prays: "The energy which creates the universe is an unparallel Almighty – *Ishwara* is that *Shakti.* He is transcendental to speech and the mind; He is eternal. His perfect ken can be experienced only by knowledge and meditation. I bow and pray unto that unknowable Supreme Being."

This divine immanence, *Ishwara,* does not work on cause-and-effect pattern. He is one with the Absolute Bliss, the *Brahman* therefore ordinarily He is not available to us, the mundane beings. Yogis and realized ones have seen Him. Who is that *Ishwara*? He is the Being; form of *Brahmā, Vishnu* and *Shiva;* the Authority for creation, existence and absorption.

The infinite energy of cosmos is beyond the range of our descriptive terminology. The foregoing brief account is only a flash of his glimpse. The *Vedas*, *Purānas, Upanishads, Gitā* and the holy treatises of all religions although give detailed narration about That but could not reach to the Ultimate.

In the opinion of *Vedas*, one may be blessed with revelation of that *Shakti* and flashes in the intellect by attaining *Samādhi.*

Thus, by meditation, there is a possibility of perceiving Him. The science has not even touched the periphery of that power. However, on the basis of scientific doctrines, the view of that infinite divine could be projected a bit clearer; of course, with a newer view point.

He is self-inspired, self-moving, and the creation of the world is also self-originated. It is not necessary to search Him, to hunt for His fountain, or the cause. He is present in every iota of the universe!

Ātman – the All Powerful

According to the Special Theory of Relativity as propounded by Albert Einstein, the Time and Space are not absolute phenomena; they are not independent factors, as it was understood hitherto. They are in unison with each other: one dimensional time and three-dimensional space. The 'existence' is possible only within the limit of these four dimensions. If any one of the axes of these four is removed: as, if we erase 'time' from the universe, then all will become zero; or if we remove the length from the space, all will vanish. These dimensions of space-time are interconnected amongst themselves and thus keeping the creation intact. It has been concluded from this study that the matter or things are nothing but energy; they are only formations of the energy.

The second famous theory of Einstein is known as 'quantum theory' according to which the energy does not exist as a solitary wave, rather it moves in the form of energy-wave bundles, named as 'quanta'. This theory reveals that basic units of the material world are atoms and minuscule particles emitted from these atoms, but they are not 'solid', rather they are the entities without forms and shapes; *Nirākār*, which sometimes appear as waves and sometimes as particles. They are there but their shape and form remains almost uncertain. And the great wonder is that their wave-like behaviour or particle-like form depends on the fact that how we 'look' at them; i.e., what we think about their shape, size or form at the time of observation; they will appear like that only. What we want to see of them? They are not *at all* 'things' yet they are only interconnections between things. The waves and the particles only exhibit their tendencies of existence. They are the wave like pattern of probabilities. In other words, they are configuration of wave-like pattern, or design, as if they are waves, but they are probabilities of apparent reality: virtual reality. It is ... but it is not!

It is thus concluded that the phenomenon within the atomic world; the facts, incidence, vision or events at the atomic level, is solely controlled by the awareness of the observer; it could be that an electron may appear as a wave or a particle; all this depends on the reaction between the 'power of the Self' of the scientist who 'looks' at them, and the electrons. It is so because electron possesses no objective attributes; that is, there is no length, width, colours or other characteristics in the electron. Such attributes are decided only by your (the observer's) *Ātman.* On reaching to this point, *Ātman* and *Prakriti* become one. Mind and matter in unison!

Clear as it is, at the subatomic level, at a finer state than that of the atom, all events or incidences occur under the influence of the Self. If wished so, all particles are converted into waves; or the reverse could as well be possible. In view of this fact, what objection stands against the description narrated in Vedas? God wished, so the universe was created! He is the infinite source of all energy and He only monitors that energy. He, at times, is perceived as energy wave – *Nirākār*, impersonal God, and if we concentrate through *Dhyān Yoga*, he also turns into *Sākār*, the personal God. We may call these states by any name, or visualize by any technique, the phenomenon remains the same.

At the ultra micro-level (atoms) and also at the mega-level (cosmos), it is the same energy, same matter and same Omnipresent Being.

Beside this, our world, our body, and our own existence – all are constituted by atoms as well as energy waves. Obviously, they are not the Reality – they are only probabilities or tendencies of being there. This mystic painting has been given the name of *Māyā* or mirage, or *Samsār.*

If you pray, with faith and sincerity, with concentrated mind and truthfulness then all will happen according to your righteous aspiration. The karma i.e., the creative energy, within the framework of natural laws, if surrendered to Him, a revelation will occur. In this way, you come face to face with *Ishwara*; the Supreme.

Creation is the Flow of Energy

The universe is filled with energy. No place is empty. This system makes the power of awareness to flow. This is live, throbbing, pulsating phenomenon. The evolution of the universe shows creative tendency; i.e., to create newer situations and then to adapt accordingly. Whether the creation aims at a predetermined purpose or goal, it is difficult to say; yet every system goes on functioning within the sphere of probabilities in conformity with the 'Grand Plan'.

Nature is creative, walks on the path of performance and achievement; it is in harmony with the flow of energy; it is progressive. All the alterations take place because the power of dynamic instinct works behind them: conviction, desire, tendency, inclination and instinct to change, to modify, to innovate and to vary; a programme to walk on the path of the creation.

We observe space with the help of various power instruments and we perceive, through calculation, the vastness, grandeur and infinitive extension of the universe; it's great, but the parameters by which we measure space and time are relatively shorter and limited in application; therefore, we are not sure about the authenticity of **those facts whatever** or which we have on record so far, whether they are absolutely true or false, or even complete or not!

We can only try to measure the oceanic water by means of a 'little pot'. But is it possible? The Time of universe is not our 'time'; the distance across the cosmos can never be our 'distance'. In this very sense, it has been narrated in the *Gitā*: the day and the night of Nature's 'wheel' and day and the night of the *Brahmāji* last for several aeons. In context to the universe, our world passes through a continuous process of alteration; it is flowing, flexible, elastic. All its vivacity is self-accelerated, tending from high level towards low level of energy. It is dynamic. The whole system is rhythmically pulsating as well as cyclic, not like a machine or an engine, rather an active, evolving, sensitive organism-like. Nature possesses the power of memory, of instinct to compete and struggle, and a capability to innovate; Nature is capable of selecting the organisms judging their fitness to survive; such a selection operates through pruning of innumerable probabilities; such 'cutting' and 'sorting' make these chances of progress simple and easy. Obviously, Nature is intelligent which applies techniques of prudence at every stage of existence. Nature functions on the basis of organized system, self-conditioning and auto-orderliness. No one commands Nature, no one arranges her components.

Nature: A Configuration of Matter and Energy

When the Infinite Cosmic Intelligence (*Brahman Pragyā*) manifests into action, it is called Divine act of *Ishwara*; the Creator. But when the same Infinite *Brahman* manifests through the medium of limited mind and intellect of beings, then it is known as *Ego or Jeeva*. Although *Brahman*, the Absolute, is reflected in both states of expression, yet one is clean and stainless and the other somewhat contaminated. However, the Cosmic Energy radiates from both, the Creator and his creation!

Prakriti (Māyā) or Nature, is inert, but *Brahman,* the cosmic awareness, is the Enlightenment, the Ken. Clearly, when *Brahman (Purush)* and *Prakriti* (Nature) are in unison, the inert *Prakriti* appears to be live and it supports the existence of living beings. For example, an electric fan is an inert object, can't even rotate by itself, but when the electric current passes through it, the activity of rotation starts immediately.

In the world, the divine energy is operative behind the 'good' and 'bad' events or things. Yet we must clearly understand that with cosmic reference the 'good' and 'bad', both have no meaning, no purport. This is only our narrow viewpoint of pain and pleasure that our ego categorizes all incidences into such states: amicable or non-amicable.

Even then, such incidences go on taking place in the flow of *Prakriti*, and their quality transmits our inclinations: that is to say, we continue to feel happy or unhappy about our world. But, in effect, the world is 'as it is'; it is as it has to be! And this whole drama continues on the immobile, infinite, immutable anvil or fulcrum.

Whatever we see and feel; that is the *matter,* the 'inert material', and by whose power this matter dances, takes birth and dies off; that is '*Brahman*'. In sum total, this is *Prakriti* or the configuration of *Mahā Māyā:* the Cosmic Illusion. It is an illusion because in reality it is there but it is not stable, not immortal and is changing every moment. Our world, our body, mind, intellect, ego go on altering every second. Therefore they are doomed to annihilation. Then how can they be infinite? They are all elements of illusion, and continuously flowing along with the stream of time and that of the cosmic energy; and we simply go on looking at that flow!

The *Gitā* Opines

Matter and energy; both are infinite; neither they are born nor die.

Matter and energy (Prakriti and Purush) both represent two facets of the Almighty. When particles (matter, Nature, Prakriti) and energy (power, Atma-tatva, awareness) meet together creation appears forth.

The 'world' with attributes converts into Cosmic Void which has no characteristics. Matter changes into energy in turn, energy changes into matter; and again matter (Prakriti) is formed. This wheel goes on revolving.

In the same way, the game of Māyā and Brahman goes on incessantly. All this happens by the Cosmic Thought of the Para Brahman.

All changes, all qualities, all forms and shapes vibrate in the structure of matter, but the Ātman is non-changeable, terra firma. All happens in the radiating light of Ātman.

It has been opined that 'cause and effect' originate from Nature (Prakriti), and hence in the transcendental state as well as at the sub–atomic level, the cause and effect become one unified factor.

The source of experience of pain and pleasure is Purusha (the Atma-tatwa), when partially veiled by ignorance.

The whole universe is born of one womb.

Every particle of matter is active and alert because of the energy contained by it.

Particles make energy by fusion and energy converts into particles by condensation – this is the wheel of birth and death. The Absolute Cosmic Energy, being constant, does not change at all.

Dimension of the Universe

Here, the meaning of 'dimension of the universe' denotes the extension of physical world as well as our 'inner world' created by our mind. The whole world is mutually interconnected; it is 'one'–not divided, not consisting of discrete entities. Our mind and the material world are united with each other.

Some mathematicians emphatically state that there are twenty-six dimensions in the universe. However, we know only four of them: length, width, height (or depth), the three dimensions of space, and one dimension of Time. The rest twenty-two expansions had curled within themselves in the form of micro-dots. What happens inside these curled dimensions is not known to us because whatever happens therein is outside of the four dimensions within which we exist. However, at times, some fraction of energy of those alien dimensions might enter the border lines of our four dimensions, i.e., of time–space, and that *guest energy* could produce such situation which we call miracle, wonderment, disconformities, or the 'act of destiny', because neither we know nor can ever understand normally, about those strange, inexplicable happenings; except at some specific state of our consciousness.

Why did it happen? How did it occur? When will it recur? All questions we ask about miracles. However, we may be able to know when our mind enters the deep meditation, when our Awareness-Self pierces through all the curbed dimensions and reaches into the transcendental sphere of existence and when our Self Energy unites with the Cosmic Awareness.

In the state of stable *Samādhi*, the brilliant flashes of divine ken could unveil all that is hidden in the curled dimensions because *the whole universe is one 'solitary organism', only one live conscious system.*

It is clear that any situation which creates 'awe' and astonishment cannot be set aside just as an 'absurdity'. Yet we must not get entwined within the confused blind faith, unscientific narrations or complex netting of religious fanaticism.

•

Resonance – 6

The whole world – living and non-living,
United by Universal Light,
Universe is throbbing, aware and alive,
Vibrating within the Infinite Might.

All are dancing on the waves of *Brahman*
In tune with the Cosmic Drum and Flute,
It ceases not, grows harsher or sweetens,
It's unbroken flow on unknown route.

Books of ken tell us the truth–
We can freely dig in for the cause,
Laws of physical world are firm,
As they swap energy and mass.

We know some rules of Nature around,
Yet, it's the iceberg's tip!
Ocean of creation thunders on,
We are floating-drowning flip.

Spirit is higher, matter is low,
Both make the illusion rife,
Lord of all moves the wheel through
Ups and downs, with smile or strife.

Sun is He, moon is He,
Plants, Planets: dwellers of the space,
Speeding atoms, beings all around,
He is breath and pain and grace

Fate may be an uncertain haze of life,
Life may be a random game of chance,
Several options on the way are there,
According to *karma*, appears the dance.

Yet, all are free to act or slouch,
Bow down at the Light of lights
Search the spark within the Self,
Perform the duties enjoy the rights.

•

Take in a Stride – 6

Continue to perceive the infinite energy of the universe by your potency of intellect.

The creator of the world has infinite forms and personal attributes. Meditate upon any one of them which harmonizes with your faith and love.

Synchronize and adapt to the situations as they come into your personal life. The practice will make your existence an abode of bliss.

Nature is the expression of *Brahman;* hence keep harmonious relation with every aspect of Nature.

Don't try to trespass the rigid line of control which delimits your intellect and never try to know, what is happening there.

Contemplate upon the formless *Brahman,* with your single-pointed mind. That power is present in every atom.

Against the backdrop of every good or bad in the world, there is only one energy, that functions.

It is your own skill, how you handle those situations.

There is no wealth greater than absolute peace, mental equilibrium, righteous karma, pleasant relationships and suitable physical fitness.

There is no success superior to giving support to destitute, contentment within, selfless service and pleasant personality.

Ascent of Spiritual Evolution

Evolution connotes progress, advancement, achieving higher state, affectivity, attainment of capability, etc., and ascent means to walk on towards newer heights with rhythmic ease.

On one hand the word *progress* refers to the process of procurement and accumulation of material luxury, worldly power, exorbitant prosperity or unlimited pleasure, and on the other, the ascent relates to the progressive journey on the road of spiritual knowledge, philosophy, cognizance of nature, *Ātman*, mind, stable peace, contentment, insight into the purpose of our life, and revelation of the Supreme.

Generally, we earn quite a lot, or at least sufficient, in our life time but we remain unable to define the purpose of our coming to this planet; always we feel lacking something; to have something more. This greed makes us to suffer.

However, it is not decried here to make effort to earn prosperity, to plan for material progress or to be self-motivated. This is not a negativity of thoughts because poverty, helplessness and weakness of all kinds are curse, a bane, or hurtfulness. If we are not hard-working and determined, the insolvency may make us a slave, and our life, while struggling against want, may go waste.

Therefore, we have to act; we must earn comfortable living and progressive standard, and also secure financial, social, life-saving systems for self as well as the family. But in spite of all this, the ascent of progressive journey may not be fulfilled! The music of life does not produce a melodious symphony. Somewhere it goes out of tune. At some corner or the other, there remains a void, and we continue to be unhappy. We still long for a stable, peaceful, simple, serene, blissful happiness!

Before analyzing the entire situation, let us critically observe both aspects, stated above.

Survival of the Fittest

– He who is the best wins!

– One who is strong, lives on for a longer time.

To become the fittest, one has to try hard for himself. No one else will do that for you. In the modern context 'fittest' does not mean to become an international boxer, rather it means to attain multifaceted development of our individuality.

For making our efforts fully effective or fruitful, it is necessary –

To define the aim of our life, in a plain and explicit way.

Not to worry about the future because the ghost of future weakens our will-power.

To plan, in a rational way, for such schemes which are logically feasible.

To remain optimistic while working in the world.

To make a policy of world wisdom for our life.

To always remember the mantra – "one day the success will greet us with a bouquet".

To keep a distance from "excess" in every field of activity.

Attempts for physical and mental fitness must be made in continuation. It is necessary to save and to earn; to maintain harmony between husband and wife; to walk on the paths of life with prudence and awareness; to adopt right methods in rearing and upbringing of children; as far as possible, to help the helpless; not to be entangled in blind-faiths or unscientific complexities of rituals. These are some blinking signals for right direction by following which we may survive the ongoing struggle and make our way ahead.

However, in addition to all these, we must be careful about our passion for high-flying, else we may become a human-machine; in this rat-race for gaining redundant wealth, it could be that other dimensions of our fulfillment may remain empty; and at the last phase of our journey all sensual "winnings" and acquisitions may appear to be worthless! Therefore, make an exact, befitting aim for life, meticulously define the methodology to achieve that aim, and work skillfully. To act dexterously is in itself high grade yoga.

While doing any work, big or small, a war-footing planning, enthusiasm to exert, and efforts in continuity are urgent. Even then, there is a chance of non-success and of a slippage at the target, which have to be kept in mind. Otherwise one may waver and flounder after walking four steps on the path.

While ascending on the path of success, several factors work together: continuous inflow of reaction; instigation or motivation from our environment of activities; support of the bedrock of our own experiences; intuition or prompting from our inner Self and serene *chitta*; our inclinations, desires or *vāsnās*, embedded within deep layers of unconscious mind; internal structure of our behavioral pattern, and our abilities or disabilities (virtues or vices) inherited by us through the genetic material of our parents and ancestors: for example, tendency of sympathy, inquisitiveness, simplicity, love, passion for collecting money or things, love for aggressive activity, etc.

To succeed in any work, following conditions are mandatory:

High degree of motivated mental setup;

High self-esteem; confidence in own capability;

Crystal clear knowledge of our achievable goal;

Maximum data and information related to the undertaking;

Facile actions to change the complexity and purpose of the target, if need be; and

Balance between work, life-style, aim and contentment.

Beside all these, it is urgent to have right emotional state of mind – an emotion which flows like a melodious background-music in the working setup.

To survive through the upheavals of life, our safety for existence is the most important factor – health, necessary wealth, security and easy inflow of fame, respect, and careful upbringing of the progeny. Beside longevity, as far as possible, a total fitness gives more happiness. Depression, tension, mental anxiety, and tit-bits of worthless worries can disrupt the balanced system of our behaviour pattern. Hence, they should be managed cleverly. We should clearly steer out of the cacti of tensions.

The moral values of life, which apparently seem to be accepted by most of the people, should be properly evaluated before adopting. The best course, however, is to create our own values by keeping our survival in view and to live every moment of life in fullness. This is not selfishness, inhuman act rather it is a natural directive.

Accomplishment of the Purpose of Life

As such, philosophically there is no justification for such questions: What is the purpose of my life? Why have I landed on this earth? Etc. It is so because after getting glimpses of infiniteness of the cosmos, omnipotence of the divine energy, quivering scenario of the world and enormity of unimaginable magnitude of ·expanses within our self and also outside of our being, such questions, as raised often, are unnecessary. Whatever is, it is. 'It is so now because it was to be so now; all is one-infinite emptiness. Then, what is the need of knowing the meaning of life? All are only a part of that cosmic form Almighty. The purpose of my existence remains as a particle in the whole purpose of creation!'

In spite of such a philosophical ken, the mind of man goes on wandering within the spheres of *Ātman, Param Ātman, Jeeva* (spirit), Nature, Divine Being, religion and spirituality; not only in the current time but since the origin of the human species.

Because of this fact, several religious paths were laid down, and millions of books have been written, and newer are being published currently, on religion and related subjects.

Let us think a bit apart from these channels:

Bewilderment or 'Theory of uncertainty' prompts or inspires the human for keeping faith in religion.

It is justified that 'belief and reason' should walk hand-in-hand.

It is required for our progress to remain aware about our own absurd and disordered thinking (or behaviour).

Whatever right and reasonable act I perform, it is the pure light of the Self which guides me to do so.

Whatever wrong and unreasonable act I do, it is the ego and desires which lead me to the spiked path.

The power of 'belief and faith' is effectively active at all times.

Miracles do occur but their cause could exist in a distant, unknown realm.

Generally, the apparent contradictions seem to be so because of difference in view points.

We are unable to perceive several phenomena yet we believe that they exist, e.g. – an electron showing either a particle character or a wave structure; consistency in the speed of light, etc.

We may be an iota or speck within the totality of the universe, yet we are a part of the Almighty.

'Probability' and 'necessity' are the two causal forces operative in the world. The cosmic energy sustains all functions. Most of the actions are invisible to us, therefore in the beginning we cannot recognize them, but when the incidents are over, then only we understand that it had happened; not before that. The search for their causes, thereafter, mostly remains illusory.

This cosmic energy is the reflection of the God; this *Shakti* remains without shape and form (*Nirākār*), and if you want to have cognizance with intent mind, it appears with a form (*Sākār*). The God is present everywhere, all the time. The energy neither lessens nor increases; the energy waves have no attributes but when they take the form of particles, they exhibit their characteristics having shape, form, measurements. In this way, the physical world, of which we are also a part, is an assembly of particles which are, in reality, constituted by energy waves. And in the end, they all merge with the cosmic energy. Nothing is born, nothing dies; all is infinite, immobile, stationary, or the 'Great Void'.

The operation of our mind, intellect, ego and life systems, are also controlled by an energy centre; we call it "*Ātman*". On one hand, this 'Self' or *Ātman* is in unison with *Ishwara* (or, so to say, it is His reflection), and on the other it is connected with the power generated by our *Chitta* (Mind in totality) and our *karma*. We feel happy or unhappy because of the un-restful state of our ego; in this process our *karmas* act as fuel. Clear as it is; if our mind, intellect and ego acquire a lasting serenity and if a stable balance could be achieved, then neither pleasure nor pain can make us shaky.

Nature is the manifestation of the Supreme Power; she arises from that power and by the same principle of *Mahākāl* (Cosmic Time) she dissolves in the Supreme. We are also a part of Nature. In varied degrees, Nature has bestowed man a freedom of *karma*, and because of this liberty to work, there remains an uncertainty or flexibility in several spheres of our working; it also means, many possibilities exist for humans to act; the field of life is not an iron jacket or firmly fixed blocks of fate.

If there were no possibilities or probabilities, or every event and incidence were firm, strongly nailed or immobile, then in that case our freedom to act would have been a zero. Think! If there would be no liberty to do *karma*, then the fruition of *karma*, ascendency in spiritual evolution, development and progress, and creation and procreation; all this would have non-functional in the world!

We understand some aspects of thoughts but several other facets of our mind are not available to us for analysis. We remain in darkness of ignorance, yet if we could know our ignorance or *Agyān*, we may become enlightened (*Gyāni*). But it is a pity that we do not understand many things, still we think that we understand everything.

Since centuries, the humanity has been entrapped in the network of negativity which the religions have been serving as a staple food: blind faith, fanaticism and deluding tall theories. There is hardly any objectivity in these paraphernalia, hence a person with discriminative intelligence must get out of these narrow lanes and by-lanes, to reach on the open highways of human welfare, support of the environment, non-violence and empathy towards poor fellow beings.

One should look beyond caste, creed, colour, country, financial disposition, religion and other discriminative parameters; it is our responsibility to redefine these man-made systems so that they could become benedictory to the humanity, and thorns of hatred embedded in our flesh could be pulled out.

Science claims to have given a lot – in many ways, our control over Nature, fulfillment of most of our needs and comforts, freedom from dark ages of ignorance, and a wider perspective of the universe. But still, science remains incapacitated to answer several questions; and while searching satisfactory solutions to our queries, we surrender to spirituality. At the same time, on the other side of the curtain, we are drowning in the redundant sensual luxury which is a curse bestowed by science!

Such a situation has created extraneous consumerism which, in the end, becomes the causal factor for our internal unrest and emptiness. For attaining lasting peace and wellness, the futility and vacuity of mechanization as well as overly consumption and wasteful exploitation of natural resources have also been exposed. Hence, the knowledge of the Self as well as *Vivek* in worldly affairs remains the only hope.

The sufferings and dejections in the world can be classified into three categories: *Ādhidaivik, Ādhibhautik* and *Ādhyātmik* the **first**, *Ādhidaivik*, is controlled by destiny, divine power or unknown forces of the universe; the **second**, *Ādhibhautik*, is monitored by the laws of physical world; and the **third**, *Ādhyātmik*, type of pains occur because of our emotional upheavals created by mind and ego.

Out of these three, we can steer out of the pains which originate within our mental sphere, but for the super mental and natural calamities we generally remain ineffective.

In view of these facts, we have to attach ourselves with the highest power who directs our activities and our thoughts. Rejecting the belief in God is to walk in the dark lanes of life leading to blind ditch. Hence, disbelief is anti-intelligence. The abode of the Almighty within our Self establishes that there exists no difference between the Creator and His Creation.

Gitā shows us the way

The foundation of the *Gitā Gyān* is *karma*. By doing action, one gets freedom. The spirituality, devotion and skilful living are also connected with *karma* or the creative energy.

One who does not perform duty, loses his path of progress, and his fame may also vanish.

अथ चेत्त्वमिमं धर्म्यं संग्रामं न करिष्यसि।
ततः स्वधर्मं कीर्तिं च हित्वा पापमवाप्स्यसि।।

(2:33)

But if you do not fight this righteous war then having abandoned your own duty and fame you shall incur sin.

Sri Krishna reminds Arjuna that he belongs to the family of warriors, and his *Dharma*, or law of living, is to fight with unscrupulous enemy, for the cause of justice, so that goodness may prevail over evil.

It is the duty of every person that he safeguards his honour, glory, repute and name and to continuously act for that. Else, the 'sin' of guilty conscious may constrain his freedom.

Infamy is always remembered; to fall from our honour and glory is worse than death.

Here are some brilliant signals for ascent

We are free to act, hence also responsible for fruits of our karma.

But the fruition is not in our hand; it remains in the womb of the future.

Don't get excited for the reward of your work.

Act, but don't get attached to that; it means never to lose the inner calmness.

Remain balanced during smooth as well as rough sailing in the sea of life.

Keeping simplicity, tranquility, and equanimity of mind is Yoga.

One gets enlightened by the knowledge of the Ātman.

It is an excellence to do any job with full skill. This also means, if one desires to progress on the path of success, one must get training for the specific work of purpose. Beside this, the highest knowledge is the "Awareness" or 'cognizance', ken or insight in every sphere of activity.

It is desirable to perform our duty with enthusiasm. It is better to be a worker than to be a sloth. To a maximum extent, we have to exert and always act to keep our body healthy and safe.

We must share, in a suitable manner, our earning with down trodden and destitute in the society, and reduce suffering in the world.

We have to distinctly identify righteous and wrongful acts. Our actions which are necessary for our development: creative and divine: are judicious; those acts which are destructive, superfluous and diabolic are ill-acts.

In the *Gitā*, the quality of various paths pertaining to devotion, *karma* and knowledge has been highlighted, yet, at times, the glory of *Gyān* has been graded to be better than other paths. It is thus evident that if revelation of the Self shines forth, the ignorance disappears like darkness in a room after lighting of a lamp.

यथैधांसि समिद्धोऽग्निर्भस्मसात्कुरुतेऽर्जुन।
ज्ञानाग्निः सर्वकर्माणि भस्मसात्कुरुते तथा।।

(4:37)

As the blazing fire reduces fuel to ashes, O Arjuna, so does the fire-of-knowledge reduce all actions to ashes.

Three types of *karma* have been identified: '*Sanchit'*, or accumulated, karma which are stored but so far un-manifested; *'Prārabdha' karma*, or the destined ones, which are being expressed in the current period; *Āgāmi karma*, or the *karma* which may bear fruits in the time to come.

Our crazy longings, egotistic desires and absurd passions become ineffective when come in contact with the original knowledge. Thereafter, mental tortures and pain-giving tides do not play havoc. Consequently, our sufferings are terminated. This is known as 'Burning of the *karma*'!

There is no method better than Gyāna to cleanse our inner self.

One, who is enlightened through yoga, is blessed with the pleasant shower of Gyāna.

When the aspirant gets plugged up with his own Ātman, at that moment the light of divine knowledge floods his intellect.

The devotee who is filled with faith; has devotion towards the Almighty and control over his senses; is blessed with *Gyāna;* and in the light of this ken, he definitely enters the realm of permanent peace.

More Directives for Forging Ahead

To keep equanimity in discomfort and comfort; not to indulge in greed; not to have excessive attachment with someone or something yet not to hate as well; to be firm-minded; and to remain composed at the time of bitter criticism; and so on. These indications are means to maintain an equivalence of mind. Extending this subject further, it has been said:

मानापमानयोरतुल्यस्तुल्यो मित्रारिपक्षयोः।
सर्वारम्भपरित्यागी गुणातीतः स उच्यते।।

(14:25)

Equipoise in honour and dishonour; the same to friends and foes, abandoning pride of doer ship in all undertakings, he is said to have crossed over or surpassed the Gunas.

For an ideal and gracious individuality, it is necessary that one keeps cool and equilibrium in a situation of both: honour and insult. The one, who develops a wider angle of perspective, is not afraid of challenges in life; one remains unperturbed and places one's ego at its right place; therefore, one continues to evolve.

Beside this, the intelligent person does not allow himself to be controlled by his ego hence he remains untouched by arrogance of a doer. Such a person remains above greed to possess more and more; consequently he is neither worried to protect his redundant wealth nor afraid of losing it.

When this *Sādhaka* achieves the highest state of knowledge and experience of the Self, he transcends all *Gunas* (*Sāttvik, Rājsik* and *Tāmsik*). Even then he continues to act in the world yet the *Gunas* cannot bind him in the rope of *karma*. During the ascent on the path of progress, following practical and simple values should be taken for adoption:

Reliability	Non-resentment
Tranquility	Non-deceptiveness
Empathy	Amicableness
Determination	Radiance of energy
Amnesty	Purity
Non-arrogance	

By following the above cited virtues, a divine serenity flows into the life of the aspirant even while living in this world, being engaged in duties, earning prosperity, name and fame and power, while caring after the family, one can adapt to the directions of *Gitā*. In the beginning, follow only one trait, the next quality will enter your being by itself. At this point, the gates of happiness will start opening.

Sri Krishna points to the magnanimity of the Supreme, after reaching where all is laid at His altar.

ईश्वरः सर्वभूतानां हृद्देशेऽर्जुन तिष्ठति।
भ्रामयन्सर्वभूतानि यन्त्रारूढ.ानि मायया।।

(18:61)

The Lord dwells in the heart of all beings; O Arjun, making them revolve, by His Māyā (illusive power) according to their karma, as if the beings were mounted on machines.

Nothing happens without the command of *Parmātman*. All takes place in His presence. Hence, it is necessary to meditate upon that power. He dwells in the inner core of all the elements. In the heart of a person who has evolved the divine attributes in his life: such as, love, patience, enthusiasm, affection, empathy, forgiveness, generosity, etc., the light of *Ishwara* shines brilliantly.

All living and non-living; meaning thereby, the whole existence, receive strength through the Cosmic Energy. The flame of our life, the Lord-in-command, is pure, infinite Awareness. He keeps the inert element of our body moving. That is the *Brahman*. That is the God. That is the *Ātman*.

Within every entity of the existence, there is a single energy that flows through; that is smeared throughout the cosmos and all energy and particles swinging on one infinite sheet, connecting them all. The *Leelā* (or play) continues; we do not understand the play, therefore we name it as *Samsār* or *Māyā*.

Yet, we are born upon this earth and Nature has bestowed the liberty to act, hence we must do progressive karma; earn prosperity, serve the helpless, live in pleasant mood, and lead a firm, unwavering, simple life.

What is the purpose of life? Decide yourself! No one else will tell you, and if at all someone may, still you will become confused, deluded.

Just try to follow what has been written in the wisdom treatises by the ancients and what has been advised by Lord Sri Krishna.

•

Symphony – 7

Every creature struggles and continuously attempts to achieve comfort, happiness and sensual fulfillment; every moment it exerts to reach to the coziness, from pain to pleasure. But in the excitement of senses, the happiness remains short-lived in humans because in that process only the senses appear to be satiated, not the intellect of the man. This 'happiness' does not concern with the glimpse of the Self. It is only – 'to eat, drink, dance, sing, heap up all that which you want for your desires, and let the ego touch the ninth cloud!'

However, to our individuality and to the ascent of our existence such happiness does not contribute at all. This satisfaction is not stable! It survives only for a while; then suddenly it vanishes! Such ups-and-downs give rise to tsunami cyclone in our mind. Oh! Achieved all, assembled every luxury, yet seems to be purposeless.

Age is advancing; near-and-dear ones are parting off, or they behave indifferently. No love anywhere; loneliness and isolation glooms around. Then, what can be done?

Alternative paths for such temporary happiness lie in the work which gives contentment, in the fulfilling activity, and in mentally quenching achievement. Such activity, which fills our being, gives something of wider meaning to life, not alone to our desire's thirst. In performing such actions which generate happiness in a wider perspective, the 'I-ness' of the doer dissolves, the boundaries of his mind disappear and he achieves unison with Absolute Bliss. The achiever, thus, clearly perceives the absurdity of stinking sensuality, and his intellect as well as *Atma-tatva* is filled with divine ecstasy.

The bodily pleasures lose their charm after some time; because of this reason, we get stuck up in the vicious circle of 'I want more', 'I want to have again'. In contrast to this situation, contentment of the Self and that of the intellect is stable as well as satisfying in which the obnoxious circle of 'want more' comes to a grinding halt.

The action of volition, or of our own choice for undertaking are those which we always wanted to perform, but could not do – travelling, pilgrimage, writing, music, painting, some service at the house-for-olds, destitute or handicapped, work for environment, meditation, fitness programme, meeting the 'long lost' friends or relatives, study of spiritual literature, worship and devotional participation, company of real sages and saints, and many more activities which provide some peace of mind as well as contentment.

Purification of Our Existence

We are always in the search of such pleasures which induce excitation, stimulation or high degree sensation. But for such a provocative 'happiness', it is impossible to stay for a long. However, alternatively, if we adopt synchronized, systematized work for judicious objective and a tranquil state of mind, then a stable happiness could be feasible,

Every person, in his life time, experiences that the circle of sensual pleasure ultimately proves to be negativity; and by holding that whirl we can reach nowhere – may remain revolving within it forever!

What we are talking about, however, does not mean that we renounce comforts and abandon all desires, live struggling with poverty and trouble. Or, we become a log.

Hence it is neither fair to annihilate all desires for pleasure and happiness, nor it is possible. Longing for safety, security, and survival is an instinct generated by Nature. It is her law to continue the show!

Once in a while, something new happens but mostly it is a run-of-the-mill life. We feel such things but do not understand clearly that if we make a bit of change in the setup of furniture, books or other arrangement, it gives a sense of feel-well, may be for a short period of time. All the more, if we could incorporate some novelty, some peculiarity, a fresh thought, some strange object or original experience, etc., in our daily living, it could be possible to feel joyous, most of the time. Such newness is lying dispersed around us, in our thoughts, and in our being.

The only drawback is that we even do not look at them. With the result, we go on treading in a groove, in a dull life-style, or on the over-used traditional ways. And generally we remain unsatisfied.

We never enjoy any situation to a full extent. Even if opportunities of joy and happiness visit us, we remain stuck up in other worries, not being involved in the fragrance of that jest and gusto. Of course, we express plastic pleasure on most of such occasions; consequently we feel a void within. If we submerge ourselves in small events of sun shine; may be for a short while, we can enjoy a swim in the flow of blissful stream. Look at the contradiction until it is not there, we are anxious to possess it, and when we encounter it, we are 'absent', mentally not present fully.

We commit mistake in looking at those tiny joys which are lying scattered around us. We do not remain alert about them: in our garden, opening of a bud into a blossom, dance of a butterfly, smile of an infant, loving look of the wife, sweet joke of the husband, rising moon at the horizon, a wave of sweet melody, expression of pleasure on the face of a hungry person after you have fed him fully, and hundreds of such situations. At least search for them; you will find many such instances.

The Absolute Bliss

In meditation, the wave-circles of mind (*Chitta Vritti*) are subsided, as has been said earlier. The secret to attain this state of mind is 'practice' with punctuality. It has been observed that when we start *Dhyāna,* it continues only for a few days; we leave it without reason. To win over this negativity, we must cultivate faith, love, devotion and surrender. Have faith; you will reach from lower to higher state of experience.

You have to elevate your awareness by intentional efforts; and the aim of such an 'effort' is to achieve a clean, pure, tranquil state of mind. It is not difficult. It is only a matter of introspection, to be fully awake and alert with *Chaitanya*. It is life!

Before us, the question is not of only pleasure, but of contentment, self-satisfaction, complacency, heart's ease by attaining which our existence could be absorbed fully in the Supreme Bliss. If we engage ourselves in the work of our inner interest, it may expand the limit of our consciousness; consequently, our mind, intellect, ego and all pain-and-pleasure will transcend across the limit of bondage, into the realm of freedom. However, even then, the worldly pleasure shall remain there but we begin to experience the trans-physical Absolute Bliss descending into our existence. The upheavals of emotions and agitating feelings will be subdued. The thought-stream of 'act for the sake of act' will start gushing; but this will happen only by performing righteous *karma*, not in doing something related to only physical sensuality or selfish gains.

Walking on the path of such *karma*, you will experience the blessings of the Almighty in all facets of life.

Thus, we may conclude; and we already know it; that the climax of happiness could not be touched only by quenching the thirst of senses; it lies in the total contentment of our being, in progressive advancement on the path of judicious *karma*, in the fulfillment of *Pursārtha,* in deep serenity, stability and consummation of our existence.

It is jeopardy that on one hand we talk about the search for true happiness and, on the other, we go on singing the absurd songs of self-admiration; we think ourselves to be greater than others, thus expose our inferiority complex by way of self-applause. If we observe our behaviour carefully, we may discover that at some juncture or the other, we are expressing our feelings of low self-esteem. or, a hazy heat of jealousy could be creating uneasiness within our mind and thoughts.

Where can one find the real pleasure amidst two lava-flows: personality anomaly of inferiority, and the bitter envy? The taste of such happiness shall remain irritable and pungent; whether we know it or not. Beside this disorder, we always exert in the search of a short-cut to earn money but we don't understand that until we know the long-way, how can we know the shortest way? In addition, the success achieved through a short-cut will not last long because we may not be able to gather needed experience of the longer walk.

We go on trying to experience quick and sharp excitements to which we name as 'pleasure'. Such stimulations create agitation and a temporary 'high', which we call 'bliss' : intoxication, sensuality, excessive consumerism, parties, blasting music, instigating outfits and costumes, unstable relationship, or other such penchant.

We make unnecessary, exorbitant purchasing under the bondage of desire. A pressure of fantasy for 'happiness' make us to go on eating mindlessly; whatever comes, we fill in; overeating. We thus attain a status of 'Sumo', obese. In that very manner, other senseless activities are prompted by our desire of indulgence in self-gratification by a short-cut, of course!

The remedy for all these illnesses is: contentment, modesty, evolvement of our existence, silence of mind, void in the self, ecstasy, offering of our life to the God, submersion in the cosmic love, justifiable *karma*, tit-bits of family pleasure and joy, aim of fulfillment, positivity of thoughts and action in the fields of our flow, and abandonment of exciting momentary glee.

Obstacles on the Path of Ascent

From a lofty peak of fascinating mountain, a small stream is flowing down with gurgling music. But on the way a huge boulder rolls down and stops in the middle of the stream, blocking its flow. For some time, of course, the trickling water stops flowing as there is no space to go ahead but, slowly, it finds a way from one side of the monstrous rock; and in due course of time, the flow of the water gathers energy of momentum and pushes the monolith downstream. The obstacle on the path is removed henceforth.

In the same manner, in our simple easy life-flow, knowingly or unknowingly several blockades enter to obstruct our progress; such hindrances could as well be the result of our childhood's impressions. This is reflected in the fact that although we know our capability to achieve certain objective, yet we only think but do not act. For example, beside our mainstream profession, some other undertaking, some small work, trying on music, writing, painting, drawing or any other hobby, training in some interesting specialized job, or studying a new subject, or practicing something of consequence could be set about.

In addition to an inactivity of not doing anything new, we generally do not fully express our affectionate, hearty, tender feelings, even to our near and dear ones. No doubt, we shake hands warmly, Oh! How are you? When did you come? All is O.K.? But has the heart touched the other heart? All is but a formality. We did not open our being, our Self! Our flow gets obstructed. Then, where is the ascent of our existence? The feeling and emotions remained frustrated. They did not blossom; they did not spread like a fountain in the mountain.

Let us see another aspect: suppose we are hard-working, industrious, motivated person, yet sometimes we could be caught up in the whirl-pool of redundancy, profusion, more-than enough syndromes. We develop a fancy and penchant towards our work, as if we were possessed by a mania to have 'more'; entwined in greed we cannot enjoy even small events of happiness with our family; what to talk of sharing a bit of our success with near-and-dear ones, or with the needy.

With the passage of time, we become a prey of mechanical or automat tendency. How can there be an evolution towards fulfillment and enlightenment?

The world is 'incomplete'; or, in other words, we see one or the other fault in the whole worldly structure. In the same way, the man is also not a perfect whole, not a complete ideal organism. Somewhere, in some way, in some form several virtues and ideal characteristics are missing. Likewise, we are not satisfied with every work or system; we see the shortcomings at a glance. But we must know that too much of critical assessment, condemnation or depreciation creates hindrance in our own progress.

We must accept this fact that we can't bring everything in order, the way we desire the world to be. Today you may feel that you have streamlined everything, but tomorrow some other oddness may arise. The main reason for such problem lies in the fact that every arrangement, each system, person or situation undergoes a process of continued alteration; the whole structure of the universe is a dynamic, power-packed, fast-shifting design, organization or scheme. This is the law of Nature. The world can't be static, stable. It is shuffling and warping; waxing and waning.

Therefore, don't waste your time in making any situation as an ideal; do only as much as it is possible to improve. Decide in a determined way; don't enter the sludge; let the flow not be hindered. If you are not able to decide, this way or that way, then sit quietly for sometime; then believing your divine flash, take the decision without delay; then see the magic! Feel the flow!

If we talk high about ourselves, the flow of progress stops by itself. People may not say anything in your presence, but at your back they make fun of you: 'very haughty, swollen-headed, bloated with pride, etc.'

Excess of day-dreaming, fantasy for achieving redundancy, or to imagine being the centre of attention of every one; all these traits play a negative role in ascent, or evolution, of your consciousness.

Then in the end, if your 'clouds of wool' do not rain, you feel miserable. Over that, if someone comments on your failure, you could be infested with a feeling of anger, hollowness, insult, shame or infamy; in sequence, you sink in hatred, jealousy, enmity, and antagonism. Anxiety and fear attack on your mental peace. This creates chain-reaction. It pushes you downwards in life and you even can't make out: 'what is happening?'

It is not very difficult; only it needs some effort. Cleanse your existence. Make it shiny. The right method to remove obstacles is to walk on, without hesitation, on ever-newer roads: aware, alert! Assemble pleasures of today, of this hour! There is no guaranty for future.

Emotional Intelligence

From amongst several types of intelligence, the worldly wisdom is necessary for practical living, to manage our life. The other intelligence is emotional intelligence. Golman (1985), the proposer of this doctrine, has defined that *"E.I. is that capability of man by the power of which he observes, feels, expresses and arranges his emotions."* This means, in addition to worldly wisdom, we must have a full cognizance of structure of our emotions: *"I am feeling angry; the anger has to be expressed but in a balanced language and controlled body language. I have to identify those causes because of which I always feel angry."*

Either fight or flee! Keep yourself in control, and seek societal support. Even then if the situation overpowers your mind, then take its full responsibility; do not set it aside casually. Neither put blame on someone else. Face boldly and squarely. Search for solution. And reassess in a definitive way. If you walk on these lines, the gushing tensions in mind will slow down.

We should never leave the hand of hope. By an optimistic view, the mind, health and intellect remain in optimum fitness and awareness. Tension, melancholy, agitations and low-feeling cannot attack. Concentrate upon the problem and focus your emotional intelligence. Then see the miracle!

You may say – "O' I also know this; I also understand this; but in practice it is not feasible." It is, no doubt. But life is yours, happiness is yours! Either be upset or be happy! We are not talking to crush or bash the thoughts; this you can't do as well. If you try, still worst thoughts will gush in with double speed! Only you have to … let them come … observe them … and let go! But, simultaneous, continue to ascend on the path of progress.

•

Resonance – 7

We are tired in the search of life's pleasure,
We are thirsty, we quench, still want abound,
We have eyes but can't see the treasure inner:
Of happiness, spilled, scattered all around.

At home, in the family, all is joy,
On the shore of good karma if we go,
Mind becomes tranquil, ego in ebb,
But acts horrid make the thorns grow.

Evolve in tune with waves of flute,
Drumming may fill with screech and whirr,
Seeds of karma are roasted by ken,
By the flame of the Self, the dynamic stir.

How can the karma sprout when burnt?
How can pain and pleasure grow?
Every atom is the abode of God,
The Cosmic Dance, the eternal show.

Make your life a blooming rose,
Walk on the lighted path of *Brahman*
Fill the Self, be tranquil and calm –
Cleanse all actions, and surrender to Him.

•

Take in a Stride – 7

1. Act to evolve your 'existence'– in progression.
2. Bliss of the Self is more satisfying than physical gratification.
3. The real joy lies in the wave-less serenity within.
4. Sprinkling of pleasantries are lying around us, look!
5. We generally miss to feel the fragrance of these tiny flowers.
6. Live fully – this moment, this hour, this day – Today!
7. Yesterday is a spent force; tomorrow is a fantasy.
8. Both are imaginations; studded with foolery.
9. Select the path of rhythmic ascent in life.
10. In the deepest realm of the heart, let the peace prevail.

Towards Nirvāna: Freedom....!

Nirvāna connotes: *Moksha*, Liberation, freedom from bondage, Infinite quietude, fearlessness, flying in the blue sky, etc. *Nirvāna* and *Moksha* should not be thought of in literal sense, i.e., word-to-word meaning. The language of religious treatises all over the world is decorated with simile, metaphors, allegory and parables. At the time of the origin of such scriptures, the populace was almost ignorant about physical and biological sciences. Therefore, based on the subjective thoughts, against the backdrop of intuitional brilliance, the ancient thinkers and wise sages have painted the beatitude of heaven, hell, *Moksha, Karma*, etc., in the form of poetry, stories, formulas to convey spiritual, moral, societal ideals and laws of life.

In the classical literature, there flows the stream of divine love, revelation, enlightenment, human psychology, experience of the Supreme, behaviour of nature and transcendental flight. However, in the modern time, contextual to scientific era, it could be uneasy to accept those descriptions literally. "Freedom from *Klesha*, clutches of *Samsār,* and attachment with our own body and the world in which we live" all this can be attained in the very life itself. Hence the picture of *Nirvāna* after the death of the body appears to be utopian because such frenzy has no solid evidence, or a physical basis.

In the modern times, 'The original sin' as described in some religious books, is only an adamant legendary which cannot be accepted today without raising eyebrows or questioning its relevance. No virtue and no power of character can be developed by a negative motivation. Of course, it could be highlighted or defined in certain terms; such as, loss of moral character, sensuality, immoral conjugal relationships, violence, terrorism, cruelty, etc., are to be taken as sins, because they create a tornado of guilt, fear, agitation, turmoil, stress, depression, hatred and other diabolic emotions in mind which are more torturous than the red hot seat of hell. They are the fruitions of 'sins'.

Thoughts and emotions: Vehicles to the freedom

The structure of thinking either takes a man into slavery or grants him freedom. The thought and emotions generally sprout from two types of specified characteristics:

Meritorious Karma:

Keeping good reputation	Cooperation	Clemency
Simplicity	Non-indulgence	

Non-meritorious Karma:

Killing	Theft	Terror-mongering.
Selfishness	Sensuality	Deceit

By performing such karma which conforms to the 'law of Nature', strength of self-confidence, optimism and faith in the Almighty evolves. We break away the chain of a hazy, undefined fear in our mind. In the end, the timidity arising from the dread of death also vanishes because of the firm situation in 'good *karma*' all through life, the heart of the practitioner remaining clean and quiet even at the time of grand departure.

This is liberation, *Nirvāna*. 'Bad Karmas' are millstone around the neck.

The spheres of positive motivation are pleasure generating. They make happiness to flow in our being by which a sense of self-contentment, added by the power of *Ātman,* dawns upon the horizon of our life. Furthermore, in a cyclic manner, the virtues, one after another, start taking roots in our existence. After these accomplishments, an aura of immutable fulfillment shines forth over the life of the *Sādhaka*. The purpose and meaning of our life is this fearlessness and freedom. *Nirvāna* is this: deep, wave-less, non-quivering, infinite peace!

To earn prosperity is desirable but to distort our life by sticking to that vicious circle is undesirable. By redundant wealth, one can get; for some time, pleasure, happiness, high-pitched gusto or tinsel fame, but unless we imbibe the ken of God, *Ātman* and Nature, these material luxuries remain mortal. A helping hand to the poor, destitute or aggrieved is more satisfying than all sensitizing gratifications. Excess of consumerism and attempt to satiate senses create some happiness, no doubt, but it behaves as if it were a mirage in the desert.

To remain sunken in the excessive materialism yet starving for spiritual elixir cannot be wisdom.

All philosophical wisdom of the world which are in search of truth and moral values point towards various paths, laws or doctrines; these indications are diversified or even contradictory to each other in some respect, but on a careful analysis it has been found that, in a wider sense, six virtues, or six paths of practicality, are common to all cultures:

1. Intellect and cognizance.
2. Courage.
3. Love and humanity.
4. Righteous act and justice.
5. Self-control, middle path.
6. Spirituality and excellence.

Intellect is another name of *Viveka* which is the quality of sharp discriminative power; through *Viveka* one can distinguish 'good' and 'evil' instantly. Such a faculty can be cultivated by practice, training and reading. A brilliant intellect of discriminative acumen widens the space for us to fly high.

Everyone understands the power of courage (including patience, bravery, daring). To develop courage for detachment from the clutches of the world is the most admirable and extremely helpful act.

Love is another name of the God. Love is a feeling or emotion which blossoms in full in the heart of all humans when one realizes His presence within. One who is overflowing with love for all can never hate, be angry, kill or keep enmity.

A person with judicious thinking can never become agitated and thus no partiality in relationship can ever happen.

Balanced, regulated way of living (*Sanyam*) is a middle path; we normally cannot control our senses in all measures because they are the media for expression of natural forces, but we can monitor and conduct their activities in a logical and rational manner. We can as well slow down our indulgence in sensual pleasures, and save ourselves from intemperance or excessive consumption.

Lastly, by entering the region of spirituality we can contemplate, meditate, read and listen about the Almighty, *Ātman, Brahman,* Nature, life, death, etc., and, thus, experience insight as well as freedom to a greater extent. Without such experienced knowledge we may always feel emptiness in our life. This is the only technique to evolve at a higher level than that of an animal; else what an animal does; we also do the same. It is also happy and so are we!

An 'animal' is a mentality: 'animalism'. It could be of the best breed, may travel in air-conditioned car, may breakfast on rich and tastiest items, but as soon as it gets a chance, it starts searching obnoxious things to eat. It must get a 'bone'; that is all. Then look at its 'animalism'.

We know medico-doctors generally come from good families. Once they are in profession, the wealth pours upon them. But, alas! At times, the 'animalism' of human mind throws all the vows of the noble profession in dustbin and begins to chew dry bones. Everyone knows, how scandalous is the 'kidney racket' involving several doctors and their agents. The poor and innocent patients suffer because of the greed of rich doctors. Such dogs ate away the kidneys, while pretending to save the life! This is a blemish on the Hippocratic Oath and a blot on humanity, as such. Man is on the path of darkness.

For advancing towards 'liberation' we must organize and rearrange our environment in which we live. We can't always live is an imaginary utopia. The problems of the world are hard to crack. First of all, be practical, face the challenges, make your day-to-day living a peaceful, pleasant music and then only attempt for liberation, or freedom.

Strong dejection, doubt, apprehension, aversion, weariness, repulsion, etc., are negativity of emotions in man. By their ignoble energy, the germinating noble traits within us also get wilted, and a stream of failure starts flowing even in our worldly activities; therefore, it has been advised by the wise that one must watch the movement of these negative shadows with *Vivek* and intent so as to perceive the direction of their dispersal. If you are alert and aware, these dark omens may meet their end by themselves.

On the other hand, the positivity of feelings, thoughts and emotions are the source of mental and physical fitness for you. One who is cheerful and lively possesses high degree of endurance to bear the sufferings in bad times, and has a skill to come out of the mire at the earliest. Evident as it is, one must remain awake towards one's safety, health and positive emotions!

If we incessantly chase 'more and still more' material luxury- rapaciously, then we may never find a path to salvation; in other words, it will be contrary to reason to hope for a freedom from pains and passion. The more you accumulate, the loftier will grow the expectation and greed! In sequel to this, the 'pleasure' of redundancy will begin to decline; then you will work harder and harder, resultantly a Himalaya of clutter may arise. But, alas! Gradually the 'taste' of rapture will again fade out! If this sequence of viciousness continues *infinitum*, when will you attain liberation?

The rich are happier than the poor only by a small degree, not too much, but we normally understand that moneyed people are very happy! It is not so! You survey and analyze yourself.

If we heap up wealth beyond the circumference of our security, we are caught up in convolution of abundance. But, after reaching to a rational level of accumulation, if we adapt to the rule of 'enough is enough', then our bondages begin to lose their grip on our psyche.

This remains a mystery: those who do not pay heed to the glow of self-enlightenment; the Sun-shine of the Supreme, and go on toiling to satiate their greed, they remain empty.

Complacency and contentedness generate that happiness and peace which equate with the ingredient of salvation. Such serenity sprouts from our clean thoughts within, less from outside affairs. Sensual pleasures are momentary hence we cannot walk on the path of *Moksha* with the support of these excitements. The world is undergoing a process of continued alteration, then how can our sensorial enhancement survive forever? As this quivering does not cease even for a second, our desire proliferates for more and more; we invent newer stimulations and intoxication of all sorts; the older ones lose their incitement! Evidently, a passion for a 'high' may delude us for life.

Therefore, the only path remains to freedom for us is to cleanse our *chitta* by practising *Manoyoga* or *Bhāvayoga*, i.e. the yoga of the mind or emotions. Live only to live at this moment (this hour and this day). Act on the directives of your intuitions when they arise from a calm and peaceful state of mind! Don't block the flow of thoughts! If some obstruction comes on the way of action, first try to remove it. The past and the future have no existence at the present moment: what remains there; it is the 'present'.

Live in the present, be cheerful, act righteously, and get connected with that cosmic energy whose one spark is within you also, and by whose power you are pulsating.

Absorb the beatitude of Nature in your being; adopt the judicious wisdom with rationale; have faith in God; practise clemency empathy, and forgiveness. Live your life lightly and in high spirit. Search the purpose of your life yourself. The freedom may greet you!

However, the question arises: what is that path? How does one feel and experience when one reaches on the highway of liberation? How can the descent of that infinite power be imbibed within? What happens when He unveils Himself and appears before us? Such questions need contemplation.

Self-realization is unparallel, the 'only one' experience; this is not a subject for reasoning which could be assessed, analyzed or praised because within its micro-vibrations and subtle waves there exists no space for our thoughts or logic to penetrate. After the revelation of the Supreme Power, the bondages of *time* are shed-off and the dimensions of *space* are diminished to cipher. We transcend all, on to the state where neither we nor He remains; both become one! The worldly riches and affluence appear to be meaningless; and one experiences the divine ecstasy as if the purpose of life has been attained!

Our mind cannot think without the substratum of 'time': remove the time, the mind will stand at zero; therefore, those spheres of our existence which extend beyond time can never be known by the mind. Mysterious and miraculous events are the manifestations of those subtle centres of power wherein our mind can never peep. Then, how can we perceive those wondrous incidences through our mind? By our gross thinking, no incidence or situation can ever originate without reason, but at the subtle plane of existence cause and effect merge together. Hence they indicate that the realm of awareness and existence is infinite. In the same way, whenever the divine energy of cosmic intelligence showers upon the being of the seeker, his *chitta* is filled with hope, bliss, light, love, beauty, grace, power and knowledge.

The *Sādhaka* (devotee) who progresses on the path of liberation looks at the upheavals and absurdity of the world with unperturbed mind. His intellect is radiating with the brilliance of blessing from the Almighty, and from his cognizance, ken, love and selfless services a rhythmic melody of life spreads out like the light of the rising sun. For him, there remains neither existence nor non-existence, nor even the mix of these two.

An unwrinkled, dynamic quietude, which fills the self with innocent delight and ecstasy, is the sign of revelation.

If we live in the present and do not stroll in the past and future too often, then our axes of 'time' come to a naught which state ferries us into the infinity. But this is possible only when we transform the way of our thinking pattern and start living afresh: clean and innocent and virtuous.

The spiritual life begins from that point when our distorted and deluded thought-flow dries up, and in its place a current of pristine stream from glacier water of love starts flowing. This is the path which leads to *Nirvāna;* this is the way to liberty!

Gitā: The Divine Flow of Freedom

Our ego; selfish mentality; and our tendencies of the past time span; it acts as speed-breaker on our way to freedom.

In the *Gitā*, this aspect has been explained explicitly:

सक्ताः कर्मण्यविद्वांसो यथा कुर्वन्ति भारत।
कुर्याद्विद्वांस्तथासक्तश्चिकीर्षुर्लोकसंग्रहम् ।।

(3:25)

As the 'ignorant' men act from attachment to action, O Bharata, so should the 'wise' men act without attachment, wishing the welfare of the world.

The ignorant toils and perspires day and night for filling the desires of his ego; on the contrary, the wise does hard work but does not get disturbed and agitated for the reward of his action, therefore he is not bonded by *karma.*

For *Nishkām Karmayoga* (Action without turmoil for fruition) some more directives are given:

- Do not work only for your selfish motto.
- Do not try to satisfy your ego in unjustified way.
- Do not worry about the future.
- Get out of the shadow of the past.

- Do not run away from the hard realities of life.
- Face the problems of the world – boldly and squarely.
- Don't be a slave of senses and mind.
- Keep a complete control on your life in your hands.

How Can one Achieve Salvation?

वीतरागभयक्रोधा मन्मया मामुपाश्रिताः।
बहवो ज्ञानतपसा पूता मद्भावमागताः।।

(4:10)

Freed from attachment, fear and anger, absorbed in Me, taking refuge in Me, purified by the fire-of-knowledge many have attained My being.

Without self discipline, no equanimity of mind could be accomplished, and without balance of mind, our aim cannot be achieved. If our mind once gets motivated to gain fulfillment or a possible higher state, then we become qualified for entering on the path of freedom. Study of scripture, continued thoughts about the All Powerful, meditation with intensive focus: by these techniques the onward journey could be facilitated. This is devotion by way of knowledge, through which we get plugged with the Absolute.

By the *karmas* which do not mint absurd desires, the doer, who discriminately analyzing his own *karma*, can never be dumped into subjection and slavery of birth-and-death cycles.

The one who remains contended with the fruition of one's action; that means, one who does not rear greed, attraction and arrogance, one who does not get entangled in the pull and push of *dwanda* (duality of opposite forces), and the one whose intellect remains unwavering during success and failure; such a person even doing vigorous actions in the world, remains free from the bondages of his *karma*. All his sufferings and sorrows wilt and wither away. He attains the highest abode.

Some More Methods to Attain the Highest Abode

योगयुक्तो विशुद्धात्मा विजितात्मा जितेन्द्रियः।
सर्वभूतात्मभूतात्मा कुर्वन्नपि न लिप्यते।।

(5:7)

He who is devoted to the Path-of-action, whose mind is quite pure, who has conquered the self, who has subdued his senses, who realizes his Self as the Self in all beings, though engaged in action is never tainted, or involved.

One who has an immaculate and unstained heart, one who is energetically hard-working, self-disciplined, skilful and seer of the Almighty Power in each particle is never chained by *karma*; thus the kingdom of liberation opens up for such a person.

- If we conquer our mind, our *Ātma-Tatva* becomes friendly to our ego; otherwise the Self (*Ātman*) may remain a passive observer.
- If one is calm and undisturbed in tussle of duality, the light of the Self guides him.
- Man can weed-out his demerits through dedication and meditation.
- Withdrawing of the *Chitta* from cobwebs of the world and then to contemplate upon the *Supreme* is *Meditation* that liberates.
- To continuously increase the power of moral rectitude and integrity, and to imbibe the values of humaneness in our being is Yoga.

Whatever great work we do, it is supported by the power greater than us. Beside this, for gaining an extra-ordinary success, one needs a helping hand of an extra-ordinary power. The one, who tries to search this path, finds it out, but one who meanders in pitch darkness, goes astray:

न मां दुष्कृतिनो मूढ़ाः प्रपद्यन्ते नराधमाः।
माययापहृतज्ञाना आसुरं भावमाश्रिताः।।

(7:15)

The evil-doer, the deluded, the fool and the lowest of men do not seek Me; they whose discrimination has been destroyed by their own delusions, follow the ways of demons.

For connecting ourselves with the very source of power, a sharp analytical intellect is mandatory which can urgently winnow and sieve '*bad karma*' from the 'good' ones.

You are free to perform noble or ignoble deeds, but remember, the responsibility to bear the bashings of the thorny fruits of obnoxious *karma* is also yours! The nature has bestowed intelligence upon you. As you like it!

जरामरणमोक्षाय मामाश्रित्य यतन्ति ये।
ते ब्रह्म तद्विदुः कृत्स्नमध्यात्मं कर्म चाखिलम्।।

(7:29)

Those who strive for liberation from old age and death taking refuge in Me; they realize in full that Brahman, the whole knowledge of the Self and all karma.

The person who walks on the path of divine life transcends all transformations and alterations going on in a flow like a hill-stream; all changes of body, mind, birth, youth, disease, ageing and death are natural sequence of events. The yogi cannot be blocked by these ticking of time. In reality, an aspirant desires to get 'dissolved' into the infinite flow of the endless Absolute Bliss. He is, thus, absolved from karma. He recognizes his Self

(*Ātman*): "This is the *Brahman*, and this is the Omnipresent". After such an awakening, he continues to work skillfully, knowing well his own *chitta*, prudence, desires, pride and the structure of life in totality.

This is Freedom. This is *Moksha*. This is *Nirvāna*!

In this context, it has been further *analyzed*:

- After the surrender of ego, the *Sādhaka* gets established in the God-Awareness.
- By focusing on the Self, the mind converges on the Ideal of seeker's faith.
- By centralizing the thought waves on the Omnipotent Lord, the yogi at the time of his grand departure merges with That power.
- One who has practised to control the senses, monitor the mind, and steer one's own energy in right direction; all through life; such a seeker integrates in Him.
- One who walks on the path of light (*gyān*) attains Liberation and the one who strides in the dark lanes (*agyān*), drops in the ditch.

Expounding on this subject, Lord Krishna narrates further:

गतिर्भर्ता प्रभुः साक्षी निवासः शरणं सुहृत्।
प्रभवः प्रलयः स्थानं निधानं बीजमव्ययम्।।

(9:18)

I am the Goal, the Supporter, the Lord, the Witness, the Abode, the Shelter, the Friend, the Origin, the Dissolution, the Foundation, the Treasure house, and the Seed Imperishable.

All attempts of our search consummate at that point where all our imperfections, wrong-doings, ignorance submerge in the experience of that Cosmic Completeness.

Our existence breaks away its boundaries and assimilates with that Boundless, and our intellect is flooded with That Light of ken, after knowing which nothing remains to be known! That truth is the abode of all, protector of all and the origin as well as terminal of all.

For making the 'basics of ascent' practicable in day-to-day living, Sri Krishna advises to arrange the fundamentals in an orderly manner:

- Knowledge is better than practice of superfluous rituals.
- Meditating upon that 'knowledge' is better than simply to have knowledge.
- To abandon anxiety about fruition of our *karma* is better than such meditation in which one remains worried about the reward.
- Renunciation of agitation about the reward of *karma* makes the stream of peace to flow.

Hence;

One who is always contended; stabilized in meditation; self-ordered; with unwavering resolute mind, and the one who surrenders to Me; is dear to Me!

The person whose *karma* or thoughts neither generate any *klesha* (suffering) in the world around nor he is dejected by absurdities of the world, he wanders fearlessly and blissfully in the spheres of happiness.

One, who remains unperturbed even by excessive gains, jealousy, fear, intensive worry, or feeling of uncertainty, becomes the custodian of stability and quiescence.

The aspirant who is in the search of a path leading to *Moksha,* or Freedom, should conserve and store the energy which continuously dissipates through the outlets of mind, speech and *karma*; he should get out of the worldly tensions and sweeping changes, while remaining connected with the **Infinite Silence** and **Immutable Divine**.

One must clearly perceive: **who gets ultimate freedom?**

He who is devoid of delusion and pride of possession; he who has a control over attachments; he who always remains abreast with the Self; he whose wild desires have been terminated; he who is least effected by worldly contradictions; and he whose mind never entertains fallacy.

These gems of divine life could be obtained by austerity.

मनःप्रसादः सौम्यत्वं मौनमात्मविनिग्रहः।
भावसंशुद्धिरित्येतत्तपो मानसमुच्यते।।

(17:16)

Serenity of mind, clean-heartedness, silence, self-control, purity of nature; these together are called 'mental austerity' (Tapa).

If we surrender ourselves, and also offer *karma* at the altar of that infinite source, from which the cosmos has originated, we could be blessed with fulfillment and be in unison with Him.

•

Symphony – 8

In the foregoing chapters we have analyzed, in brief, all that by way of which we may lessen the pains of our mind and also the spasms. In the current chapter we have known about 'freedom' and the ways to attain it.

From every node of 'knowledge' several shoots sprout which develop into new branches and, again, from these twigs many more secondary branching ramify; this process of leteral spreading of knowledge has been continued since millennia. Such an organization of secondary and tertiary branching has resulted into an enormous tree of knowledge under the shade of which we are blissfully breathing today.

For mundane persons, like us, who do not like to be lost in the jungle of meanings, grammar, diagnoses, descriptions and contradictions of interpretation, all this may sound to be complicated and unintelligible. To fish out the meaning of simile, metaphor and allegory is the job of expert critics of the subject. Those worldly people who are entwined in the cobwebs of their family and relationships generally avoid to involve in deeper investigation.

Still, we are inquisitive to know – how our pains and suffering could be diminished and declined?

The only way to solve this tangle is to walk from complexity towards simplicity. You must have learnt, read or listened a lot in your life, but even then the element of the real 'knowledge' remained convoluted and undulated! Hence, straighten out and chisel to make your ken shine; then by this brilliant cognizance enlighten your life and make your individuality a cultured and noble ideal.

It is your existence, not of anyone else! Let us think further in this context.

Characteristics of an Enlightened Person

Generally, we live in the shadow of a hazy fear of death, which deepens during a serious illness or encroaching old age. "If I leave this body, what will happen to my wife, or my husband? This work remains undone, that desire could not be fulfilled, etc. Such thoughts thunder again and again. Future appears as darkness. Belief in next birth is there, but that too is not firm. No desire to remember God, or no interest in meditation! Wealth, passion, love, longings create a terror that they are being left behind, and despondency about an infinite emptiness of the future.

It is a general situation in which humans find themselves when terrorized by death.

On the contrary, the person who is filled with celestial knowledge remains in quietude. He contemplates upon the All Powerful God, and sheds off worldly attachment. For him, the death is merely a continuity of the journey from one level to another; a transformation, an enlargement of the circle, and a change of dimension. He does not tremble and flutter by the terror of discarding this corpse.

The Characteristic of a *Siddha Purush*

Our spheres of living are generally small; our thoughts are not liberal and our mind remains conditioned. We generally do not become large-hearted, open-minded, liberal and empathetic. If someone has criticized us, it pricks deep within; we keep that pain and grudge for the whole life. Forgiveness, clemency, consolation, generous thoughts nothing of this sort come to last.

The enlightened person, the *Siddha Purush* wanders freely outside of these narrow lanes, under the blue sky of infinite extent. He always remains intimate to full life. He is not a close-minded creature. He cheerfully acts and lives through all aspects of his existence and consummates them. The balanced person earns wealth, enjoys comforts, abides by values of good life and virtues; and then, at the last run he abandons all to become detached, dispassionate conscious being. Such a yogi is welcomed to the land of freedom. But only he who has practised non- attachment throughout his life, can do so at the last phase.

Generally, whatever we study at school, college or university, we get satisfied with that and take it for 'knowledge'. We are happy; earning bread-and-butter, then what is the need for learning more? The person with this mind-set remains as a water body in a pot-hole. Neither a fresh flow enters it, nor spread out to gain more water. It stinks and dries up in summer.

On the contrary, an enlightened yogi accomplishes all that learning which is worth acquiring. He does so by contemplation, meditation, reading and keen observation. He prunes-off absurd information and entangled branches of the worldly superfluity. Thus he accumulates only the essence of 'Truth'.

Usually, we think that if we have to live in this world, struggling with day-to-day problems and to run the family smoothly, then the knowledge of only practical use is required, not the philosophy of renunciation. This thinking sounds sensible, but we perhaps do not realize that a person whose life is suitably regulated, who practises *Dhyān Yoga*, and studies intently, generally acquires abundant insight and glimmer of ken, besides an effective control on worldly affairs. It is so because the mind of the *Gyāni* remains unraveled; he has an insight about the formation of his desires and he is established in the deep *tranquility* at the innermost realm of his being. All these are the special endowments for a successful person, who feeds the body and fulfills the needs of spirit.

Constant bashing of the world splits our personality; producing a speedy alternating thought flow! A gush of worries and troubles keeps the concentration in abeyance. The mind will always jump and do monkey-tricks, yet the seeker whose knowledge is blessed with divine light, keeps his mind in focus upon the present; this moment, this hour, this day. Not always on the past or the future. Except for the current time, the other realms of the time remain a 'void' for the one that is prudent. He grows well and controls everything equally well.

In brief: if we want to imbibe and assimilate our 'knowledge' in a facile manner, we have to adopt the following, methods: *freedom from the fear of death, an ongoing effort to become large-hearted, continued study of the scripture, rearing of a sharp Viveka and penance for concentrating the mind.*

Power of Mind and the Grace of God

Power of mind and grace of God relates to those aspects of our *Mānas Urjā* (mental energy) by which our 'existence' could be connected with the *Parm Ātman.* It must be discussed in a simple way as summary without complicating it any more.

- Our mind is divided in many layers: unconscious, subconscious and conscious. Also, our ego and superego remain active. We call an assembly of all these factors as *Chitta.*
- All appendages of our mind and its various strata are confined within the four dimensions of time-space. This system can become active only within the limits of these four walls; not across that.
- In *Dhyān Yoga,* first of all we observe, with a sharp-edged awareness, the upwelling thoughts which originate from the *chitta.*
- We have already seen in the Chapter on *Dhyān-Yoga* that to calm down the *Chitta Vritti* (the spreading circles of thoughts originating from the mind) is known as meditation.
- We contemplate upon our 'ideal' (deity), mantra, revered name, personified form of a power centre, a spark of beam of light, or our Guru.

- By repeated practice with patience, a deep concentration starts prevailing by which the waves of mind become motionless, and spontaneously our 'existence' transcends the boundary of the time-space.
- This is transcendence, exaltation, enshrinement, trans-time, sublime, supra-mental, beyond the world of our experience and an ecstasy of consciousness.
- At this point of our highest flight, when we merge our being with the Supreme Being, the revelation of the *Brahman*, the Absolute, happens.
- *Brahman* is Energy Supreme, Power of Cosmic Dynamics, and Bliss Absolute. In the very experienced bliss, there lies the golden womb of the universe.
- In this yoga-like state, the limits of our mind and body get dissolved, the bondages disappear and our 'existence' attains salvation: the *Moksha.* Our ego and super ego also vapourize; we become one with the Absolute Brahman.

Our aim of life is this. There is no happiness greater than this state. There is no achievement bigger than this. Rest is nonentity. In the initial stage of practice, we may remain in this state only for a short time, but by-and-by the seasoning increases and the 'light' intensifies; so also the time of our *Samādhi* (absorption) prolongs. After continued practice for a long time a stage comes when effortlessly, at any time, we enter the intense *Dhyāna* and swim in the sea of blissful trance. We forever remain blessed thereafter.

We do not 'get'; we 'become'. We break away the confinement of time and fly, as a liberated bird, in the infinite blue of heaven. Even doing *karma*, we are not bonded by the *karma*.

The awareness shines forth in our intellect. No worry about past or the future. The 'present' takes over our life. All tsunami tornados subside and a power of tolerance and endurance sprouts in our individuality.

Paths of Science and 'Knowledge'

Here we are talking about 'science' as material science and 'knowledge' as *Adhyātmic* knowledge (spirituality).

Scientific research has cleanly washed away several blind faiths of humankind during the last two centuries. It has also contributed immensely in raising the standard of living, comforts and fulfilled innumerable basic material needs of man. However, the so-called negative situations supposedly produced by science are not the misdeeds of science itself; they are the result of wrong approach of humans themselves. For example, science has invented atomic energy for the betterment of the society but the use of atom bomb is left to the prudence of man. You may use a knife for your day-to-day work or cut-off your own nose! Science is only responsible for making a good, sharp knife! That is it.

Science is based on the fundamental methodology of 'cause and effect'; there is no place for emotions, virtues or faiths in this approach. On the other hand, spirituality is a search of relationship between our spirit, because of which we are alive, and the Supreme Power.

Here, the linear system of cause and effect breaks down because both the factors merge together. But again, unfortunately, in the religion; which has been the main source of spirituality for centuries; several absurdities and contradictions have grown like mushrooms: rituals, fanaticism, non-rational style of thinking and ignorance in varied shades.

Therefore, it is the need of the time to adopt suitable scientific approach in *Dharma* (religion in narrow sense) and *Adhyatmik gyān* (Self knowledge). By doing so, the panorama of our views shall extend. The blind beliefs can as well be removed by asking questions, doubting the theories, searching the root cause, adapting to rationale and skeptic approach, and to see the things with an open mind.

The essence of this approach is that if we give some freedom to our thoughts for wandering into scientific spheres, and then we continue to practise our *Sādhnā* (devotion, yoga, etc.), the contradictions and conflicts between science and religion will not arise.

A brilliant intellect and *Vivek* are born from insightful perceptive experience as well as dynamics of the *chitta.* Thus, knowledge and discriminative power in combination with the experiences of our whole life can usher us into the righteous path because ***knowledge*** *is generated by study;* ***contemplation*** *spreads the glow of Vivek; and* ***experience*** *makes the structure of our own world.* We must synchronize or at least sincerely try to synchronize these three musical instruments of life energy.

Alteration of Consciousness is Liberation

What is the ultimate freedom, *Nirvāna*? *Detachment from traction, liberation from blind faith, end of the fear of insecurity, and independence from loathness are ultimate freedom.*

And Still More:

We must break-up the mental imprisonment; show determination to achieve higher goal: Transformation of total personality; Cleansing of awareness; Ordered monitoring of the ego. For it we must abide by the truthfulness; achieve nearness to God through meditation; take the responsibility of all our acts; and sensitize, be more aware of divine power within through righteousness in karma.

Keeping these directives as pointers, make your own philosophy. Determine the standard of *karma* yourself. Be responsible for your maximum progress.

Nature has blessed you with a freedom to act and to think in all possible directions; now it is in your hands to make use of that liberty in a sensible way. Freedom to perform *karma* does not mean that you walk on degraded path, or for satiation of your wild desires you adopt undisciplined and immoral behaviour. On the contrary, it means, do your *karma* taking them to be your duty and remain intimately connected with the Supreme.

•

Resonance – 8

Mind is chained – hands and feet,
It can't pull the passion's nail,
Gates are locked, desirers on watch,
Foul, sensuous walls of hell.

Light of knowledge: flickering frail,
Dark are shadows on the heart,
Only when the divine invoked –
Shackles of *Māyā* break apart!

Blinking, fluttering world of man,
A great 'Mirage' – so we name,
From womb of mother, till today –
How much change! Never the same.

Searching pleasure: night and day,
Where lies bliss in sensual race?
Fulfillment abides in *karmas* righteous;
Look into the Self, then shines the Grace!

Open your mind's wings in sky,
Fly ... fly through Eternal Glow,
Shed-off ego's layer of stink!
Let the fragrance of *karma* blow!

Be in penance, intense, austere,
So as to terror of death subdue,
Enter another horizon of time
Pure, peaceful, eternal blue!

See the reason, and the effect,
Act with total power-build,
Earn, and learn pleasure and pain,
All the corners of existence filled.

Search the knot in unconscious mind,
Meditate deeply to knots untie,
Across the time and beyond the space:
Let the mind be pure and high.

Live all moments: 'now and here'
Not in the future, nor in the past,
Today of 'now' is infinite, incessant,
'Today' represents the cosmic time, vast.

Sufferance of tsunamis: a shadow in mind,
Light of insight can heal the pain,
Look! And 'let it go' in flow,
Sorrows could be eased by grace and ken.

•

Take in a stride – 8

Detachment from the *Samsār* is *Moksha.*

Right or wrong deeds generate peace or worries.

Follow the six practical ways which are universally recognized as effective.

Nurture your positive emotions and energetic motives.

If we are aware about the 'present', we may experience the ecstasy of the cosmic time.

To remain in happiness, be optimistic.

Look at the shuffling world with an unperturbed mind.

The path of diabolic traits dismantles our serenity in life.

From the network of mingled webs of learning, search simple and easy way for your use.

It is your life. Glorify, or make it garbage! As you wish?

But since you are a human being, the best creation of the Almighty Brahman, so be human, sublime and divine. Glorify yourself and your Creator.

Also Available in Hindi

Also Available in Hindi

Also Availab in Kannada, Ta

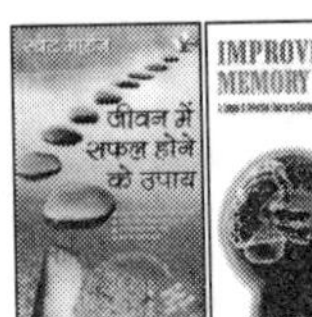

Also Available in Kannada

Also Availabl in Kannada